Glass Fusing
in a
Clay Kiln

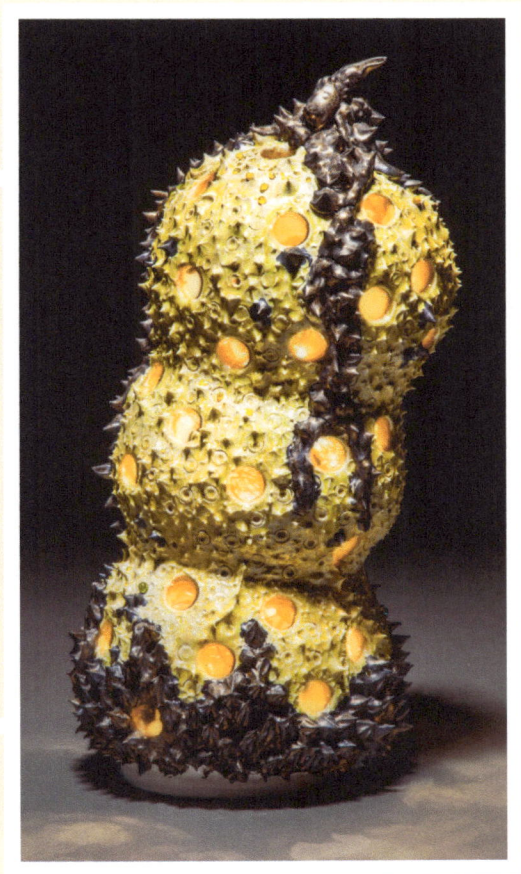

Lisa G. Westheimer

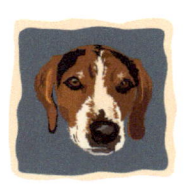

PeTeY PIe PresS
WWW.PeTeYPIePresS.COM
62 GLeN AVeNue
WesT OraNGe, NJ 07052
973-996-8115

for permissions and usage contact
Lisa G Westheimer
lisa@lisagw.com

ISBN 978-0-9841007-6-7

Design by Rich Sheinaus, Gotham Design
gothamdesign.com

DEDICATION

My journey as a creative and educator is not solitary. This book is dedicated to my beloved husband Bill Westheimer; to administrators Martha Kelshaw and Kate Hutson, and fellow glass instructor Peg Kenselaar at the Yard School of Art at Montclair Art Museum; ditto to Kristin Muller, Jennifer Apgar and Beth Schwartz at Peters Valley School of Craft. I also dedicate this book to all of my students in all my classes and workshops, especially my masters students who have been with me through thick and thin from the very beginning: Ronni Pressman, Katie Stillman, Pat Provost and Richard Sheinaus. Lastly, in dedication to my dear Professor at Montclair State University, William McCreath, I reiterate: **THIS IS ALL YOUR FAULT!**

TABLE OF CONTENTS

INTRODUCTION

I have a Masters degree in ceramics. My skill in glass fusing is self-taught through trial and error. The information I am about to impart may conflict with or be different from your experiences or those that you have heard from other glass artists or found on the internet. Find what works for you using what information you have gleaned from books, Internet, other artists, workshops and most importantly your own trial, error and tests. Take excellent notes and pay attention to what does and does not work. Glass is an expensive medium, but it can be recycled endlessly just by following a few simple rules.

Every studio artist searches for ways to maximize their existing studio inventory; save money, time, effort and studio space. Expanding into the medium of glass does not have to break the bank or create a major disruption to a ceramic studio. Electric ceramic kilns can be used to fire glass with pros and cons that are found through trial and error. Knowing your ceramic kiln- its hot and cool spots can maximize your glass making, and knowing what added wear and tear can result will help you care for your kiln and its components.

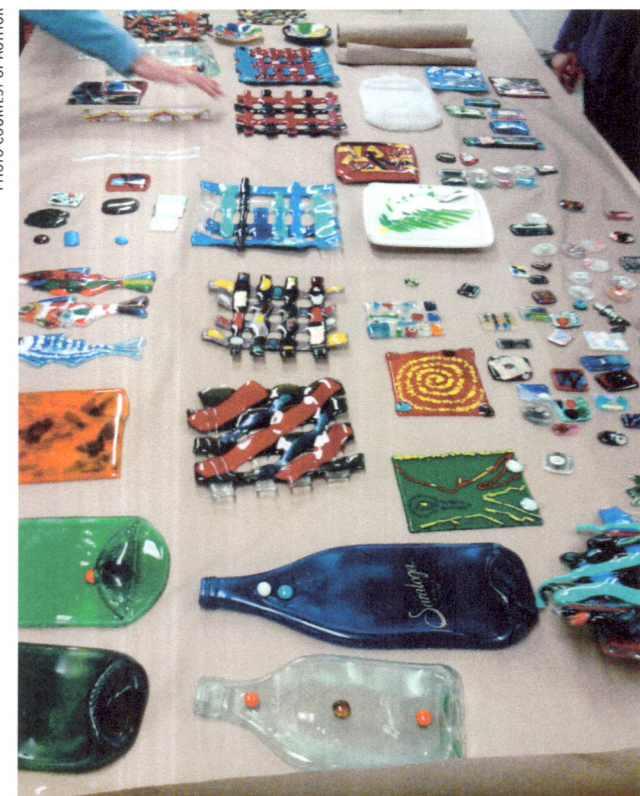

Fulled fused, tack and slump fired glassware

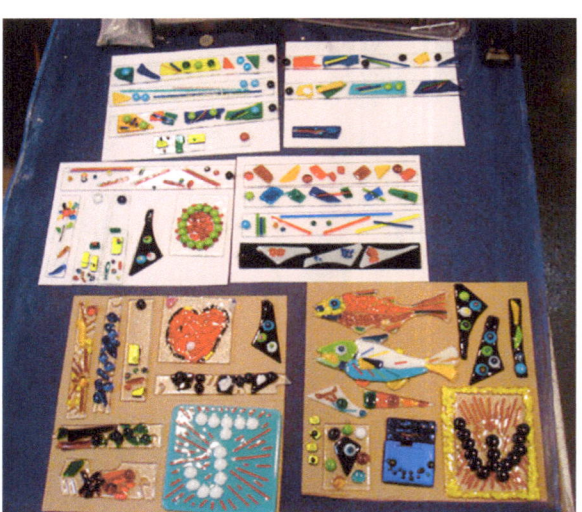

Tack fired student work

EQUIPMENT AND MATERIALS TO GET STARTED

Kilns:

Glass kilns are usually shallow. Many have elements in the lid or the base. Ceramic kilns are usually more vertical with elements along the sides, many vented with enviro-vents and equipped with digital controllers. I fire glass in my Skutt 1027 with a digital controller and enviro-vent system, I purchased this kiln in 1997 and through diligent care and maintenance successfully fire both clay and glass on a continuous basis. Mainly, I replace my thermocouple every 100 firings and try not to fire in the glass temperature range for more than 10 weeks at a stretch without firing at clay temperatures in between. There will be more on this later.

Kiln furniture:

Full sized, very smooth kiln shelves are recommended, as the firing of glass in its liquid state it will pick up any cracks, seams or imperfections in your shelves. Half shelves are recommended for those times where all full shelves are in use and you need cover shelves for the load, or when you are working small.

A variety of posts in all different heights are recommended.

Fiber (refractory) rigid board and flexible paper:

Glass *can* sit on a kiln-washed shelf, but the kiln wash must be thickly applied and as stated before, glass will pick up any imperfection in your shelf, from dings to cracks to level changes in kiln wash thickness, even brush strokes. I have found using a combination of rigid fiber refractory board with flexible refractory paper on top works very well to ensure a smooth surface no matter what condition your shelves are in, and saves having to add kiln wash more often than needed in firing ceramics.

Kiln wash:

Make sure all of your shelves are scraped and kiln washed regularly to protect them from any glass that comes into contact with them. Vacuum your shelves with a vacuum equipped with a HEPA filter regularly, or you will be very sorry when your glass and glazed clay creations have "kiln poop" (rough white flakes of kiln wash) fused into them.

Ceramic kiln wash and glass kiln wash have different properties, but are basically a mixture of alumina hydrate and kaolin. I have not had a lot of luck firing glass directly on kiln washed shelves no matter if the wash is for clay or glass or how thickly it is applied. I find it much easier on my kiln and on myself to cover my shelves with rigid fiberboard cut to fit the shelves, with a single layer of flexible fiber paper on top of it. The rigid fiberboard is reusable; I have gotten about 100 firings out of a single sheet before it gets brittle and falls apart. Flexible fiber paper is single use; it turns into a powder after firing, BUT I find that if I am doing more than 1 load of full fusing in a row, I can reuse this set up at least twice, thereby exacting an attractive savings on money, time and effort. I simply remove them from the shelf and set them aside (horizontally) until the next firing or leave on the shelves and set those aside (horizontally.) Make sure you have room to do this and note it is friable so handle wearing gloves and a mask and run your air filter.

Rigid fiberboard/thick kiln shelf paper:

As stated, it is reusable. Typically glass can be fired directly on it, but I have found that the glass in a liquefied state cannot move the way it needs to on rigid fiber board; that if the glass is fired too hot or held at temperature too long, it will form a sharp, serrated edge in the cooling process which requires grinding (extra time and effort) and a fire polish (extra firing, time, money, effort) to remove. It also sticks to the bottom of the glass; and requires scrubbing and leaves a texture that is sometimes unpleasant, depending on the look and texture you want. I buy it in bulk and cut it into sheets to fit the size and shape of my full shelves, using the scrap in my smaller kiln or under ceramic ware in a glaze fire in lieu of stilts, sandwich between glass sheets to create a hole, I even use it as shims in my kiln and to sit ware on in my raku kiln. It has lots of uses. IT IS FRIABLE SO USE GLOVES, AND MASK AND RUN YOUR STUDIO AIR FILTER WHEN HANDLING. Store the rigid fiberboard in the original box standing upright. Discard when it becomes brittle.

Flexible fiber/thin fire paper:

This comes in paper sheets that you can cut easily to fit your entire kiln shelf or to sit under a small, single piece of glass. It is not reusable; it turns into a powder. IT IS FRIABLE SO USE GLOVES, AND MASK AND RUN YOUR STUDIO AIR FILTER WHEN HANDLING. For storage roll up in paper or plastic and place horizontally.

SWITCHING BACK INTO CLAY MODE:

Try to schedule glass firings in a group so that switching back into clay mode is worth the time and effort. It is essential to clean the kiln thoroughly to get rid of any friable materials left by the rigid board & fiber paper and any kiln wash that may have come loose during the firings.

This is what I do when using both rigid board and flexible paper:

1. Place a garbage can near the kiln
2. Turn on the studio air filter
3. Put on gloves and a dust mask
4. Have a putty scraper and damp sponges handy
5. Remove the shelves one by one
6. Remove the rigid fiberboard and hold it over the garbage can so the dust from the flexible paper falls off, delicately use the scraper if you have to.
7. Store the rigid board standing upright in its box
8. Wipe down the kiln shelf including sides with the damp sponge, clean sponge as you go
9. Store the kiln shelf (I stand mine upright.)
10. Repeat until all shelves are done
11. Vacuum the kiln thoroughly, bottom, sides, elements, using a vacuum with a HEPA filter

If I am running a glaze firing directly after a glass firing I will run my envirovent with the kiln empty overnight to further remove any particles left in the kiln.

When using only fiber paper on the kiln shelf I simply remove each shelf, hold over the garbage can, scrape off the powder with a putty scraper, damp sponge and store the shelf.

Shelf maintenance:

When cleaning, observe how well the kiln wash is wearing on each shelf. I try to scrape and re-apply kiln wash when I notice the existing wash is peeling away, and especially when I have a big important ceramic glaze load about to go in.

Kiln maintenance:

I started teaching 10-week session glass fusing classes, doing all the firings in my clay kiln, 2 to 3 a week, at temperatures ranging from 1325F to 1480F sometimes 1525F. I noticed during the first year that the bottom elements in the kiln were starting to bulge. I wasn't worried because they were the original elements and the kiln by that time was 20 years old. After replacing the elements, I noticed after another year that they were starting to bulge again. I take meticulous notes when it comes to firings: date, temperature, cone, ramp/hold, hold times, # of hours it took, what was in the load and how it was stacked, results. I also number the firing from when I replace the thermocouple and replace at or around the 100th firing. (my notes show that the firings start to have problems around this magic number.) I also take note when I replaced the elements. Take notes and find your kiln's magic numbers.

My kiln repairman suggested that the elements were bulging because I was firing *too low* for *too many firings in a row*. He suggested I fire at least to a Cone 06 bisque firing, preferable and Cone 5 – 7 firing in between to mix things up to "fluff up" the elements, i.e. have them get hot enough for them to conform to the shape of the grooves. That has caused me to mix up my teaching schedule, alternating glass and clay sessions so my kiln gets a break from the lower temperature ranges. This may or may not happen to you and you may get funny looks from the people you trust to maintain your kiln and this may conflict with what you read on line but it works for me.

Firing Schedules:

Firing schedules and temperatures will depend on several factors: tectonics, annealing/quartz inversion, coefficient of expansion/contraction (COE,) and what result you are seeking: full fuse, tack/dimensional/contour, slumping, fire polish, pot melt. Many of these principles overlap with ceramics, especially in glaze firing. Consider learning these nuances as if you are fluent in 1 romance language and trying to learn another: many of the rules are the same just with a different accent and sometimes a different order or meaning. I have found that being proficient in glass firing has made me better at glaze, raku and luster firing.

Using witness cones:

I am a bit of a cone queen when it comes to my clay practice. I use witness cones all the time in all temperature ranges to see if my clays/glazes/lusters have reached maturity. I typically don't use cones in my glass practice mainly because the temperature ranges of my kiln for optimal results do not have a specific cone temperature AND over the years, like in raku, I have learned to judge maturity by sight. Use cones if you need to in the very beginning until you get adept at judging by sight if your results meet expectations.

Basically there are 6 ways to fire glass in a kiln:

1. **Full fuse**: When you want the glass to liquefy to turn multiple layers into 1 flat solid sheet. In my experience, glass likes to seek 1 level and the magic number of layers to seek that level is 3, about ¼" thick in total. So if you want to combine colors to create 1 smooth, solid, even layer of glass do not exceed 3 layers. NOTE: embellishments, even if they do not cover the entire surface, equal 1 layer.

   In my art making, I typically use a base layer of solid (opal) colored glass, a layer of transparent (cathedral) or clear glass cut to fit on top and then put embellishments of decorative glass dispersed on top. I have found that if I place these embellishments too close to the edge, i.e. within 1/8" of the edge, it will bulge and I will not have a straight edge on that side, so I avoid doing that. Many glass artists will teach you to sandwich the embellishments between the bottom layer and top layer of glass. This does not work for me as 1) I have to travel over many speed bumps to get my student work from the classroom to my studio to fire and the top layer gets jarred loose; and 2) I find that the vibrations from my envirovent can cause the top layer of glass to slide out of true if it is not resting directly on the base glass layer. Experiment and do what works for you.

   Full fuse firing range: Depends on what type of glass you are melting. Found glass/bottle glass/float glass/window glass/wire glass typically melts at a higher temperature than glass manufactured for the purpose of fusing/hot working, usually in the range of 1460F to 1525F. **NOTE NEVER EVER EVER FIRE TEMPERED GLASS IN YOUR KILN, IT WILL EXPLODE. BE VERY CAREFUL IN EXPERIMENTING WITH FOUND GLASS!**

   Fusible "hot glass," i.e. glass manufactured specifically for fusing typically fuses at a lower temperature, in the 1450 – 1484F range, depending on COE and manufacturer.

2. **Tack/dimensional/contour:** when you want the glass to stick together but want to maintain texture and shape of the individual pieces: 1400+/-F

3. **Slumping:** when you have a full fused sheet of glass and want to form it into a specific shape like a tray or dish by sitting it on a mold: 1320+/-F

4. **Fire Polish:** when you want to remove scratches or grinding marks without affecting the shape or texture: 1375+/-F

5. **Bubble Squeeze:** this firing is long and expensive but well worth it. It is just what it says. It has a very long hold time at 1250F on its way up to target temp to extract as many gas bubbles from between the layers of glass as possible, creating a very smooth finish. It takes around 20 hours to fire, not including cooling to unloading temp. Note that it is usually not practical/cost effective for teaching environments as it takes too long and it is better to spend the money on supplies than kiln costs.

6. **Pot melts:** this is a really fun way to recycle glass of compatible COE. It needs to be fired really fast and really hot, in the 1600F range. Basically you place glass shards in a clay flowerpot balanced on posts, run the kiln hot and fast until the molten glass flows out the hole in the bottom of the pot and forms a colorful swirly pool on the protected

kiln shelf. It will eat up your rigid fiberboard, and the glass will be thick and harder to cut, so keep that in mind, but it's really fun.

NOTE: Every kiln is different and testing is essential to find the correct temperatures that work in your kiln. Note that glass is very sensitive and finicky, you will need to adjust these temperatures and your hold times depending on how the kiln is loaded, i.e. if it is packed full or has lots of air around the ware, and how evenly your kiln fires. I find I have to adjust my temperatures as my thermocouple ages and especially when I replace it. TAKE METICULOUS NOTES!

Some basic firing rules:

1. ALWAYS ALWAYS have a cover shelf in the kiln, especially those equipped with envi-rovents. This will help with heat conduction and ensure the top layer of ware is not exposed to circulating air, it will force the air to circulate down the sides of the kiln and away from the ware and will help it heat and cool evenly.

2. Glass loads fire most evenly when they are packed full. My Skutt 1027 likes to have 4 shelves of ware, but I have done 3 or 5 in a pinch. If you must fire a small load in a large kiln pack it full of furniture and molds in the bare spots, and use 4 shelves, pack blank shelves with furniture/molds and use a cover shelf.

3. Find the cool spots in your kiln. Note that they change, especially when you change thermocouples: 2 thermocouples ago my kiln's cool spot was the lowest shelf. Now it is the highest. Kilns are like cats, the minute you figure them out they change. TAKE NOTES!

4. Use the cool spots to your advantage: sometimes you can fire 2 different types of loads at once, i.e. full fuse on your hot shelves and tack on your cool shelves, or combine a slump and fire polish firing in one load. Saves time, effort and money!

5. Take meticulous notes. Keep a log, record how you packed the kiln (how many shelves, how much ware) how long it fired, hold times, # firings since last thermocouple installed and results.

6. ALWAYS unload the kiln when it has reached room temperature or at least within 20F room temperature. Most glaze firings are ok to unload after 100F; glass is not. A good way to ruin a lot of expensive hard work is to crack open the kiln before it is completely cool, with an emphasis on the word crack.

THE SCIENCE OF GLASS

a) Tectonics/Annealing:

Clay, glaze and glass have some basic similarities in molecular structure and the movement of same at quartz inversion and liquefaction temperatures. The best way to visualize this complicated notion on a grand scale is tectonic plates in the Earth's crust pushing against or pulling away from each other during earthquakes. Cracks in the Earth's surface form when 2 plates pull away from each other; mountains form when they crash into each other. In the case of glaze and glass, which are very similar in molecular formula as they are silica based, cracks can form in the heating and cooling process (thermal shock,) and uniformity is created depending on quartz inversion within the 800 – 1000F temperature range either heating up or cooling down.

Visualize glass molecules to be like pieces of a puzzle. In full fusing you are attempting to take several pieces that have never fit together and make them interlock perfectly. As in quartz inversion during glaze firing, in the range of 800 – 1000F, molecules begin to float around and intermingle. Once they reach their target temperature, to get all the chemicals and their molecular structures to combine and fit together, they need to cool back down to that range. Glass needs a lot more time to do this than glaze or clay. It needs to go through the *annealing* process- wherein it is cooled from target temperature down to about 960F and held there between 50 and 60 minutes to allow all the pieces of the molecular puzzle to fit perfectly and permanently.

I learned this concept the hard way when I was experimenting in glass fusing. I placed circles of window glass in slumping molds and slumped them to the target temperature recommended. I had no clue as to firing schedules and didn't know what annealing was, but they came out perfectly and I felt like a genius and gave them as gifts to friends. I learned over time from my sheepish friends that every single one of them broke for different reasons: one exploded on top of a TV (this was before flat screens.) Another one shattered for no reason other than the sun shining on it on their dining room table. What I learned the hard way was that because the glass was not annealed, the molecules were reacting to the subtle changes in temperature caused by the sun/TV and literally pulling the pieces apart.

b) Coefficient of Expansion/Contraction (COE:)

As important as annealing is glass compatibility. Not only does glass need to be annealed, all of its components must expand, contract, and anneal at the same rate. Every glass manufacturer uses different recipes in making their glass. These subtle differences literally make or break the results of fusing. When combining different bits of glass for fusing, they must have the same coefficient of expansion, or COE. This is a mathematical calculation of the rate in which the molecules move in heating or cooling. Don't ask me for the calculation—it is way beyond me. Do not mess around with mixing COE's unless you are making fine art and going for that fractured look. If you are making functional ware and you overlook this, you will be sorry. Typical COE's are 84 and 80 (Murano glass and many rods used for lamp working) 90 (Bullseye glass is the most common) and 96 (Spectrum 96, Wissmach, Youghiogheny and Oceanside to name a few.) Basically, use the same COE from the same manufacturer and you will be fine.

Flotsam
2009
Glass, metal, lucite
19" diameter x 6" h

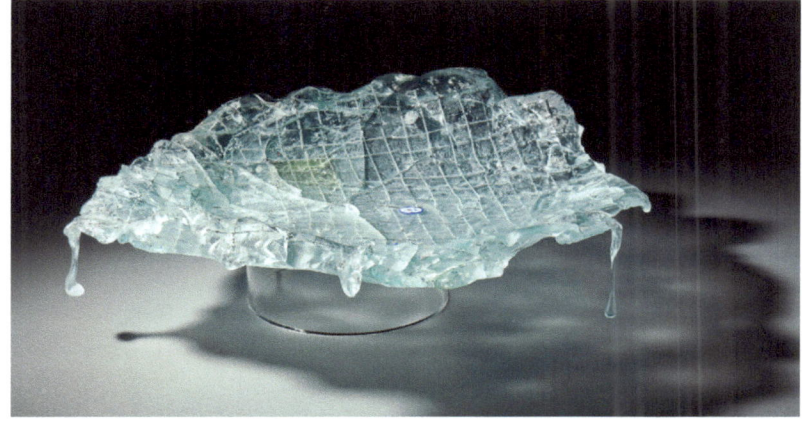

A little story: *Spectrum System 96 hot glass used to be manufactured on the west coast of the United States, until 2016 when it ran into issues meeting EPA standards. The company, its recipes and much of its equipment was purchased by a company called Oceanside and operations moved to Mexico. Oceanside began producing COE 96 glass to replace System 96 in 2017. It is experiencing some compatibility issues, and also manufacturing issues such that some components like pebbles and mille fiori are not available and it sometimes has issues melting with other COE 96 glass from other companies like Uroboros or Wissmach that System 96 was always compatible with. So once again, take notes and if you have issues, contact your supplier and let them know, they are actively seeking this information to help produce quality product. Problems will resolve over time, as the factory gets up to speed.*

Since I have always worked in Spectrum System 96 COE 96 glass I intend to continue until either my supplies run out or they get back up to speed whichever comes first. Choose whichever glass you want but stick with it but do not mix COE's.

c) Found glass/Bottle glass/Window glass/Wire glass/Stained glass:

If you like to tinker these are for you. If I am looking for ways to procrastinate from working on my ceramic projects I either will develop a new glaze or try to find the correct temperature to melt found glass, i.e. glass I did not buy from a fusible supplier with a known COE. What got me into glass fusing in the first place was a piece of shattered wire glass I was given as part of a collective project where participating artists were given detritus from a targeted California wildfire. We were asked to make art out of it and return it to be sold at auction to help those impacted by the fire. After agreeing to participate and shoe box arrived at my door, containing a piece of wire glass window that had shattered so badly in the fire that the packer simply rolled it up and put it in the box for mailing.

I didn't know what I was doing at all, but I had melted window glass to 1525F in a mold that was kiln washed that looked like it was made of porcelain that had holes in it, so I set about making a bisque terracotta clay mold for the glass to sit in.

It was free form so in addition to kiln washing the mold I put 1" thick refractory blanket in it and let it and the wire glass drape over the side. I added a handful of mille fiori slices I had picked up in Murano, Italy along with some fragments of lampworking rods that were too short to use that a fellow artist gave me. By that time I knew what annealing was all about so I put it all in the kiln and kissed it up to God. And thus the sculpture *Flotsam* was born (see image above). The results were magical and I was forever after hooked.

The beauty of working with the wire glass is that it doesn't matter if it fractures, the wire holds it together, so adding incompatible components isn't as much of an issue as found in other types of glass.

Basically, in working with glass of unknown COE:

1. Take a lot of notes
2. Use the firing range of 1465F – 1525F and fire incrementally, i.e. every 10 degrees, either working your way up or down within the range to find what works. Too cool and it looks tack fired; too hot and it will have serrated edges. Once you find the range you can mess around with hold times and bubble squeeze, but have fun with it and be patient.

SETTING UP YOUR STUDIO TO WORK IN GLASS

Clay and glass can co-exist in your studio, but unless you have separate rooms for them, not at the same time. I have a small studio and my solution is to have all my glass supplies in covered bins on dollies with wheels. On top of the bins go my large equipment and cutting tools. All my clay is stored in covered bins on wheels as well. So when it is time to work in glass all the clay goes in their bins and wheeled under the counters while the glass bins and equipment get wheeled out and put in place. I cover all my work surfaces with disposable recycled paper and throw it away before switching over to clay again. I wipe down all surfaces with a wet sponge wrapped in paper towel so the sponge does not get impregnated with glass fragments. I also damp mop the floor.

STUDIO SAFETY

It is essential for your safety that you do not work in glass and clay at the same time in your studio. Glass can shed tiny fragments in cutting that can get onto your wedging board, into your clay and reclaim buckets. If you work in glass in a clay studio you must NEVER EVER put floor sweepings in your reclaim bucket and you should have dedicated sponges for cleaning surfaces, AND wrap them in paper towel before wetting and wiping so that any glass fragments get tossed away with the used paper towel instead of in your hands and fingers. A Swiffer Mop™ with disposable pads work well for cleaning the floor of glass shards. I also tell my students to wear closed toed shoes, no sandals. Cutting yourself is par for the course when working in glass so I have a steady supply of Band-Aids™ on hand. But nothing is worse than getting a tiny shard in a finger, hand, foot or toe that is invisible to the naked eye, especially when one wants to throw clay the next day.

Cutting glass can cause fragments to go airborne so always wear safety glasses when cutting, grinding and sawing.

Inhaling powdered glass/fiber paper is also a health hazard, so basic safety measures must be taken to protect oneself: make sure your grinder and saw have enough water in them and add water to it if powder or paste forms; wear a dust mask; run your air filter while working.

STORING GLASS

Glass is as expensive as it is fragile so care should be taken in handling and storage for safety sake and to protect your investment. Glass should never be stored exposed in a studio where someone can walk into it or accidentally touch it and get cut. Glass becomes difficult to cut when it is cold, I have had it shatter or cut unevenly leaving tiny shards when taken from an unheated storage room during winter, so I recommend storing it in a climate controlled room. It likes to be stored vertically to prevent breakage. Handle it carefully so as not to cause flaws that can make it fail when cutting.

TOOLS, EQUIPMENT, MISCELLANEA

Some basic tools you should have on hand, many items are ceramic studio staples:

1. Kiln wash (I find the kind for clay is just fine) and a dedicated brush for same
2. Rigid fiber board (at least 4 sheets)
3. Fiber paper (expensive, try to buy in bulk or on sale)
4. Refractory blanket (for working in large sculpture)
5. Cotton swabs (Q-tips™)
6. Cotton pads (the kind found in cosmetic aisles of stores)
7. Glass cleaner (Everclear™ grain alcohol found in liquor stores is best)
8. Pistol grip glass cutter (to score the glass)
9. Glass running pliers (to break the glass along the score line)
10. Mosaic tile nippers (make sure they work with the thickness of glass you have) (these "nip" little bites of glass along the score line)
11. Glass grinder (expensive, you can get away with using a dremel™ if you have diamond bits, you can use a dremel™ to drill holes too)
12. Morton system/Portable Glass Shop™ with cutting board (expensive and you can do without it but it is very worth it and the board catches glass crumbs for easy retrieval/disposal)
13. Scrubby pads (sponge on one side, abrasive on the other)
14. Sharpie™ pen (not fine line)
15. White Sharpie™ pen (for marking black opal glass)
16. Ruler
17. Water source
18. Nitrile gloves
19. Terry cotton gloves
20. E6000 glue™
21. Elmer's glue™ (the white kind works better than the clear)
22. Needle nose pliers
23. Tweezers in various lengths
24. Magnifying lens or eyewear
25. Dust mask
26. Protective eyewear
27. Bins with lids to store glass preferably on wheels
28. Sectioned storage boxes or recycled small, lidded containers to store bits of glass and findings.
29. Clear nail polish
30. Nichrome wire

Fancy expensive stuff:

1. **Circle cutter** if you dare (they take some practice and waste a lot of glass in the learning curve.) You can also buy pre-cut circles in various dimensions, expensive but wasted glass from failed cutting attempts add up.
2. **Bottle cutter** (they are even worse to use than circle cutters but once you get the hang of them they can be an asset)
3. **Glass saw** (they are expensive and temperamental, invest in only if you want to do detailed precision cutting and don't mind the expense and the care they need)

Some of the greatest strengths clay people have are their ability to adapt, recycle and reuse and their proclivity towards miserliness. These traits should be deployed when buying glass and glass supplies. You can go crazy in a glass store buying all sorts of things you probably have or don't need so take an inventory of your clay studio before you go nuts in the store or on line. Make a list of supplies before you get in the car or log in to shop. If you go to the supplier in person take someone with you to take things you don't need out of your cart or slap your hand when you reach for something not on the list.

And for heaven's sake stay out of the kiln aisle! Many suppliers have notoriously faulty search engines as well as affordable odds and ends in stock that aren't on the website so if you can make a trip, go. Many have bins of scrap glass by COE that is sold by the pound that can be a real money saver. Note that if you are unlike me and are adept at production pottery and good at precise slab working you can make your own molds rather than buy them. They are very expensive and fragile and need to be maintained, so making your own out of your own stock of clay as needed, can be fun and cost effective.

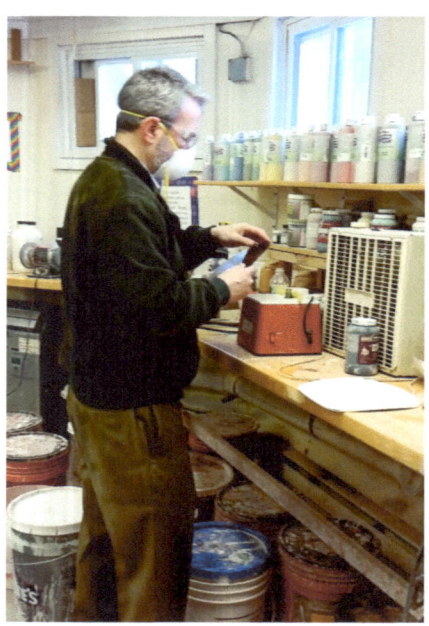

Student Richard Sheinaus working at the grinder

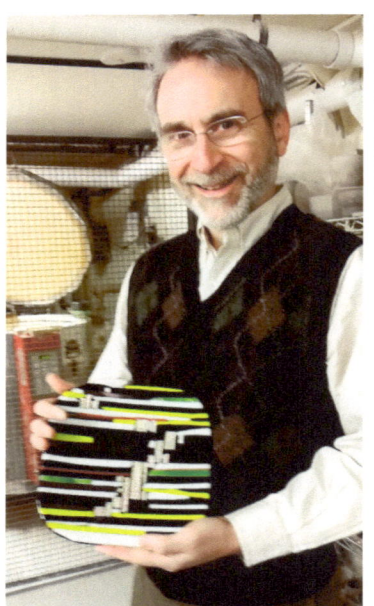

Sheinaus with one of his signature creations

PHOTO COURTESY OF AUTHOR

PHOTO COURTESY OF AUTHOR

LET THE FUN BEGIN: GETTING STARTED

Choosing which hot glass to full fuse:

Personally, I like my full fused glass to have 3 components: an opaque (opal) base layer, a clear or transparent (cathedral) layer over that, and decorative bits of colored glass (embellishments) on top.

Opaque (opal) glass vs translucent (cathedral) glass:

Remember reading the nuances between ceramics and glass and how they are like 2 different romance languages? Well this is an example. Opal/opalescent means "opaque" in glass language but is called "lustrous" in ceramic language. Opal is just another way to say opaque. As stated previously, opal glass maintains its color after firing. what you see is generally what you get, unless you are buying glass that "strikes" a different color, i.e. changes a definite other color after firing. Glass that strikes is clearly advertised and marked as such, just make sure you keep it that way when you store it in your studio.

I can only guess that translucent glass is called "cathedral" for its use in stained glass.

Opal glass is more dense and rigid in the kiln. It does not move as much as cathedral glass. I have found that fusing 2 pieces of cathedral glass gets a different result than fusing a layer of opal with a layer of cathedral on top. I find that when slumping cathedral glass, it moves a lot more than opal, and can sometimes distort and result in misshapen ware, so be aware. If this happens in your kiln and you still want to slump only translucent glass try lowering the temperature incrementally until you get the result you want.

Fusing 2 pieces of different colored opal glass will just get you 2 layers of the 2 colors you started out with, so be aware. Fusing 2 pieces of colored cathedral glass will result in a color according to the color wheel, so be aware of that too.

Fusing a piece of colored cathedral glass on top of a dark color of opal glass, especially black will usually waste the colored cathedral glass. So if you are thinking of doing this test it on jewelry sized pieces first.

DECORATIVE PIECES:

Noodles and Stringers:

These are long rods of colored (opal) or transparent (cathedral) glass of various thicknesses and shapes. I call them by pasta/noodle shapes:

- **Udon:** Thick round rods. Makes a thick straight line when fused or rounded line when tacked. They can also be broken up into slices that can be fired flat to make dot circles.

- **Linguini:** flat rods that look exactly like linguini pasta, make a straight line when fused, a flat raised line when tacked.

- **Cappellini:** thin rods that make a straight line with fused at exact temperature or tacked, or squiggly line if over fired.

Udon thickness is usually how mille fiori start out before they are cut into slices. More on mille fiori later. You can score udon then break it by hitting or crunching with nippers, linguini and cappelini can be broken apart easily to desired lengths with your fingers or nippers.

Mille Fiori /Murini:

Originally made in Murano, Italy, before Venice became a tourist destination and drove all the factories to China. Basically long rods of layered multicolored glass. Artisans using their expertise assemble them so that when these rods are sliced a design is revealed inside i.e. a flower, symbol, animal, etc. Search the internet to find videos of how this is done; it is impressive. After the rods are made they are cut into slices. Placing these slices horizontally and full fusing will cause them to melt into little pictures. They are very pretty. COE 84 from Murano has the best colors in my opinion. Recent factory made 96 mille fiori are disappointing in their color range and clarity. I have found some artisans that still make them and make them out of COE 96 and buy them directly from them. They are EXPENSIVE, usually sold by weight or amount, but very worth it.

Dichroic:

Dichroic glass has metallic that when melted produces spectacular results: it glows, shimmers and changes color. Dichroic usually has a black opaque (opal) backing that produces a black outline when melted; or are clear and produce an iridescence. Many are textured for tack firing. Cabochon for jewelry making can be made simply by cutting and melting it on its own. Dichroic is wildly expensive, some are $30 an ounce or more. The fastest way to waste your money is to put the metallic side facing down rather than up when firing or assembling with other glass.

Pebbles:

Pebbles are melted drops of glass that when melted form a circle. They come in opaque (opal) and transparent (cathedral) and some "strike" a different color than they look before firing, i.e. some clear or amber pebbles will strike/turn opaque/opal orange in fusing. READ THE BAG. COE 96 pebbles are very limited in range as of this writing, as Oceanside does not have the equipment to make them yet. Pebbles can be made simply by cutting small squares of glass or breaking up udon rods into slices and melting them at full fuse on their own in the kiln.

Frit:

Frit is ground glass or glass fragments. It comes in various grits: powdered (for using stencils/enameling) fine, medium and coarse grits. Use them to accent or draw a design in glue using a cotton swab and sprinkle it on the piece and tap off the excess (use one color at a time, catching the excess in a paper plate and return to the bottle one color at a time or you will be sorry!)

Coarse frit is handy to make flowers petals or waves or sunrays rather than cutting it from a sheet of glass. Frit is also the crumbs you produce in your glass cutting, fyi.

As a rule I do not permit the use of powdered frit in my studio or class room for environmental and health reasons. It is easy to get everywhere and get in eyes and fingers, mouths and lungs. Many glass artists who work in it work in special ventilated stations that resemble spray booths. If you have a spray booth I bet you can use it.

Iridescent:

Iridescent glass has a subtle coating of metallic on one side that shimmers and changes color in the light, like an opal luster glaze. It is difficult without a specific machine to determine which side is the metallic side, so hold it up to the light, move it around and do your best. Usually the side with the label on it is the metallic side. If you remove the label mark it in pen. Note that when metallic side is FACING UP it forms a skin that will cause any glass on top of it to TACK fire- i.e. embellishments will not completely sink into it. Iridescent FACING DOWN when placed on a base layer of glass gives a pleasing semi glossy crinkly opalescent look to the piece and any components placed on top (clear side up) will sink in completely. Do your best.

Some basic rules in assembling hot glass components:

1. Opals go on the bottom, clears/cathedrals go on top of opal, and decorative embellishments go on top.
2. Opals stay their true color no matter what.
3. When mixing 2 different transparent/cathedral colors they will change color according to the color wheel.
4. Do not place a colored transparent/cathedral over a black opaque/opal, the color will be wasted and so will your money.
5. If you are selling, use dichroic and iridescent sparingly, the market usually will not allow you to charge accordingly in terms of jewelry and small functional ware.
6. Metallic side of dichroic always face up.
7. Placing glass components over dichroic or iridescent will cause them to tack fire, but sometimes clear will give it nice smooth 3 dimensional look.
8. If you want a straight edge after a full fuse do not place components too close to the edge, set them back at least 1/8".

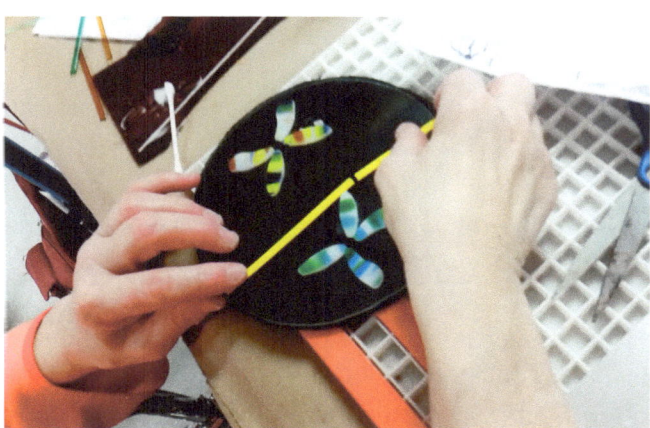

Assembling glass for full fusing and slumping

PHOTO COURTESY OF AUTHOR

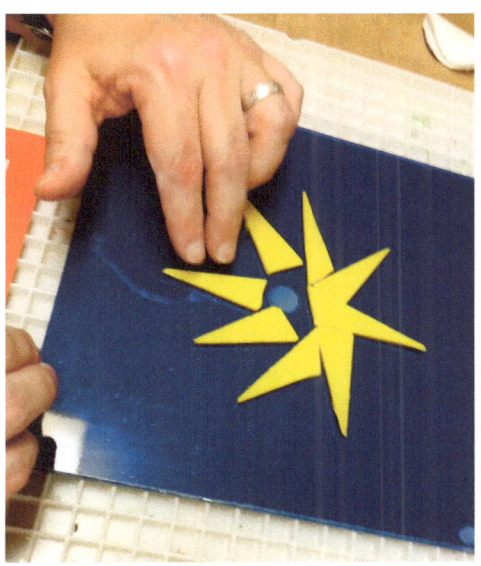

PHOTO COURTESY OF AUTHOR

CUTTING GLASS

There is a knack to cutting glass but once you get the hang of it it's easy. There are a few very basic rules. Science wise, by scoring the glass you are interrupting the molecular structure in the tectonics of the surface, making a weak spot, that when hit, will break apart. You want to be committed and definite in your scoring- 1 pass and 1 pass only; and you want to hear a "scratching" sound as you score. Score all the way from top to bottom as best you can, but it is most important that you apply even pressure all the way.

Using a Morton System™:

A Morton system™ consists of a plastic grid of squares that you plug components from their Portable Glass Shop™ into that assist and guide you in cutting glass in a straight line or on a diagonal into shapes, very handy for stained glass. Not only does the grid allow you to plug in various components, it allows you to catch the broken bits of glass for use as frit. It is costly and comes with a dvd/manual/training videos to help you learn how to use it. They have excellent customer service. I use mine as I do my brain— to a fraction of its capabilities, but it's terrific for cutting glass accurately and quickly.

To cut glass using a Morton System/Portable Glass Shop™:

NOTE: I have my glass sheets cut into 12"x12" pieces. They fit in the bin and in my Morton System™ at this size.

1. Choose the glass you want to cut
2. Measure and mark the glass
3. Set up the Morton system™: place the large squaring fence at the bottom, the squaring block at the top and secure the cutting bar to both.
4. Place the glass under the cutting bar, resting on the squaring fence and place marks you made against the cutting bar
5. Hold the pistol grip cutter so the blade is touching the glass at an angle where it is lower at your wrist than at the cutting wheel.
6. Pressing firmly, make ONE AND ONLY ONE CONTINOUS pass over the glass from top to bottom using the cutting bar as a guide. Make sure your efforts make a "scratching" noise. ONLY SCORE ONCE, DO NOT GO OVER WHERE YOU MISSED.
7. Turn over the glass. I rest ½ of it on the cutting bar with the score side facing towards the plastic grid surface on an angle. This will help if break along the score.
8. Turn the pistol grip over and repeatedly strike the glass along the score with the metal end (remember the score side is facing down so with opal glass you are doing it blindly) Keep hitting it until it breaks or you are sure it won't.
9. If it does not break on its own, turn it over, line up the running pliers along the score line and squeeze as if you are squeezing a hardboiled egg.

NOTE: If you do not have a Morton System™ you can cut the glass by resting the cutter against a ruler and using a folded towel, soft catalogue or magazine as a base, then turn the glass over and hit it with metal on the opposite end of the cutter and PRESS DOWN HARD with your fingers along the score line.

Cutting circles:

Circles take finesse so practice on scrap glass first. I use a circle cutter. I like the kind that can fasten onto the glass via suction and have rulers for easy measuring. Make sure the blades are sharp, replace as needed. You can get them in various sizes. Set the circle cutter onto the glass. Use a piece that is slightly bigger than the circle you want to cut, no more than an inch larger in all directions.

1. Measure out the desired size and tighten the cutter arm.
2. Score the circle, try to maintain a constant pressure, do not go over the score line, and just complete the circle.
3. Remove the cutter from the glass.
4. Using a pistol grip cutter, score a line in every corner of the glass beginning at the circle score line going out to the edge of the glass.
5. Do the same ½ way in between each corner on all 4 sides of the glass.
6. If the piece of glass you are working with is large you may need to make more score lines along the sides. TRY NOT TO SCORE INSIDE THE CIRCLE SCORE LINE.
7. Turn the glass over and tap along the circle score line with the metal end of the pistol grip cutter. Keep doing this and watch for the score line to fracture. Take care not to fracture the circle.
8. Once the glass has fractured all the way around, if it has not released, turn it over and gently press along the fracture lines to release the glass. Use running pliers or a nipper when necessary to get it to release completely.
9. If it does not release cleanly you can remove nibs with a nipper or by grinding.

NOTE: the scrap shapes left over from the circle cutting are great for making jewelry or embellishments on large projects.

NOTE: There also is a way to cut them using the Morton System™ and some additional equipment, check out the video: https://vimeo.com/245735081/99050a8c7d

NOTE: Check out how to set up and use the Morton System™ and the components of the Portable Glass Shop™ provided by Mortonglass.com by viewing these videos:

PG01B - Portable Glass Shop:

- **Glass Shop Basics** - Video (https://vimeo.com/247842865/f064fb2618)
- **Glass Shop Angles 1** - Video (https://vimeo.com/254231311/ee956e4c4c)
- **Glass Shop Angles 2** - Video (https://vimeo.com/259774531/bbf1b7bba3)
- **Cutter Slide** - Video (https://vimeo.com/48904044/1516cd63b3)

NOTE: Check out these videos on suggestion of tools and their proper use provided by Mortonglass.com:

Understanding The Safety Break - Video https://vimeo.com/228111285/3c4e41491b

Toyo Glass Cutters:

- **Toyo Pistol Grip** - Video (https://vimeo.com/215904000/dd90868ebd)
- **Toyo Custom Grip** - Video (https://vimeo.com/215903966/256006fafd)

Cutting glass without a Morton System™:

Believe it or not, before the invention of Morton Systems™ it was possible to cut glass. It requires a bit of skill and patience but practicing on scrap glass will help. All you need is a steady hand, a pistol grip cutter, a soft surface like a magazine or folded towel, and glass running pliers or nippers.

1. **Cutting straight edges** simply place the glass upon the soft surface, hold a ruler to it and score along the ruler edge. Turn over on a soft surface (see **NOTE** bottom of page 18) and tap along the score line with the metal end of the pistol grip cutter until it breaks. If it doesn't, press down on the score line until it breaks. If it doesn't, turn over and use the running pliers to break it.

2. **Cutting circles**, use a circle cutter to score the glass to the desired circumference. Score a line from the circle score out to the edge of the glass on every corner and in the middle of the glass sheet. Turn over onto a soft surface and tap, tap, tap along the score lines. Be very aware to avoid tapping on the score lines radiating out from the circle so as not to have the fractures continue into the circle. Turn over and press long the circle score line to break. If it does not use the running pliers, be very, very careful not to fracture the circle.

3. **Cutting free form shapes**, draw the desired shape in marker on the glass. Score along the lines pushing away from you, slowly and carefully, taking your time. Try not to saw away with the cutter. When you have gone all the way around, score a line from the score line to the edge of the glass the way you would for cutting circles. Follow the instructions above for breaking the shape away from the rest of the glass.

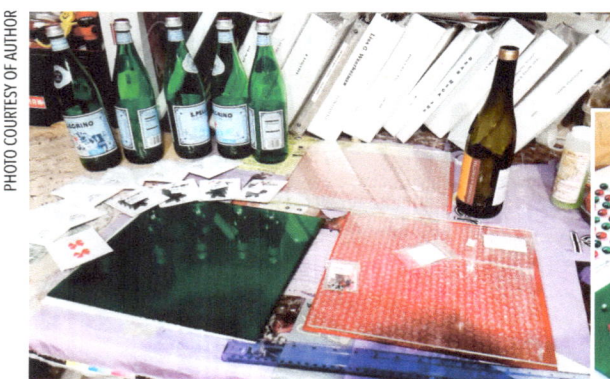

Bottles, sheets of glass and glass cut outs ready to be processed for firing

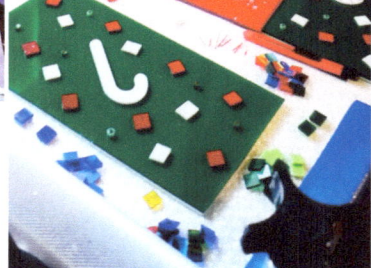

Cut and assembled work ready for the kiln

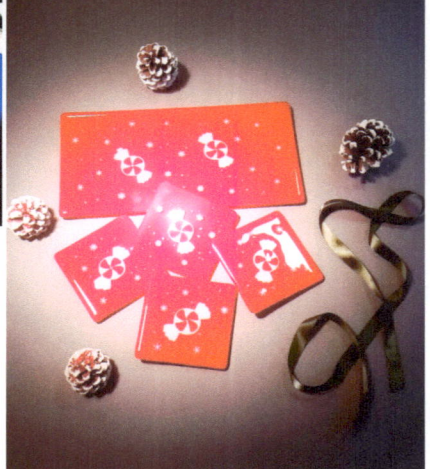

The finished product ready for sale

ASSEMBLING GLASS COMPONENTS FOR FIRING

1. Stack the opal and cathedral glass with opal as the base layer, (or 2 cathedrals if you wish) one on top of the other.

2. If you are transporting your glass over any distance on its way to the kiln, let's say another room, before stacking the glass, dip a cotton swab/Q-tip™ in a bit of Elmer's glue™ and place a small dot of glue in each corner of the base glass DO NOT USE TOO MUCH GLUE OTHERWISE IT WILL CAUSE A BUBBLE AND A GREY ASH IN BETWEEN THE 2 PIECES OF GLASS.

3. Once you have placed the 2nd layer on top of the base, arrange the decorative components on top of the 2nd layer, gluing with a small amount of glue as you go.

4. NOTE: when using frit you can dip the swab in glue and use it to "paint" a design on the top layer of glass, then placing the glass on top of a piece or paper or a paper plate, sprinkle the frit on top of the glue with a spoon. Use 1 color at a time, tapping off the excess onto the paper/paper plate and using the paper/paper plate to return each color to its respective bottle as you go.

5. Place in the kiln that has been set up with rigid fiber paper/thin fire paper set up, or just thin fire.

Where to place your work in the kiln:

After you have learned the hot and cool spots in your kiln, use them to your advantage. Place items that you wish to completely full fuse in the hot spots, and place the items that you want to tack or have texture/contour in the cool spots. For example, you have assembled glass components to make a functional glass plate. You want that to be flat so that food or cutlery does not catch on any of its surface. Make sure to put it in a very hot spot in the kiln so that it full fuses into one flat sheet. Or, if you are making a fine art piece where the design would benefit from texture, or making jewelry where you want to maintain a specific shape, place it in the cool part of the kiln to tack/contour fire. Make sure the glass rests on the fiber paper/thin fire paper. Work which is comprised solely of cathedral glass can fire cooler than opal glass, so that can go on a cool shelf too.

Fire up the kiln according to the desired schedule. The following are schedules that I have developed over the years from what I have found on line and in books. Use them as suggestions, through testing you will find the correct schedules for your kiln.

FIRING SCHEDULES:

FOR SYSTEM 96 AND COE 96 COMPATIBLE GLASS

Glass Full Fuse Firing Schedule

SEGMENT:	RAMP TEMP/HR:	GOAL TEMP:	HOLD TIME:
1	325 F	1000 F	10 minutes
2	600	1465-1484	20
3	9999	960	50
4	150	700	10

(target temperature about cone 015)

Glass Slumping Firing Schedule

SEGMENT:	RAMP TEMP/HR:	GOAL TEMP:	HOLD TIME:
1	325 F	1000 F	10 minutes
2	600	1320-1325	25
3	9999	960	50
4	150	400	10

(target temperature about cone 018)

Glass Tack/Contour/Dimensional Firing Schedule
(bonds glass together but leaves detail of individual pieces)

SEGMENT:	RAMP TEMP/HR:	GOAL TEMP:	HOLD TIME:
1	325 F	1000 F	10 minutes
2	600	1400	20
3	9999	960	50
4	150	700	10

(target temperature about cone 016 or less)

Glass Fire Polish:
(brightens work and removes scratches after grinding and finish work performed)

SEGMENT:	RAMP TEMP/HR:	GOAL TEMP:	HOLD TIME:
1	325 F	1000 F	10 minutes
2	600	1350-1375	20
3	9999	960	50
4	150	700	10

(target temperature about cone 017)

FOR FLOAT, WINDOW, PANE, BOTTLE GLASS:

Glass Full Fuse/Slump Firing Schedule

SEGMENT:	RAMP TEMP/HR:	GOAL TEMP:	HOLD TIME:
1	325 F	1000 F	10 minutes
2	600	1500-1536	10
3	9999	960	50
4	150	700	10

(target temperature about cone 013)

POT-MELTS (MAKE SURE TO PROTECT YOUR SHELVES VERY WELL!)

SEGMENT:	RAMP TEMP/HR:	GOAL TEMP:	HOLD TIME:
1	600	1650 F	90 minutes
2	9999	960	60

Make sure to keep a log. It's best to write down the following information:

- Date
- # of firings since change of thermocouple
- # of firings since change of elements
- Type of load:
- how many shelves,
- what type of work,
- how was it packed: full every shelf? Did you include any kiln furniture to further pack the load? Were any of the shelves full of just kiln furniture? Did you put a cover shelf? (yes you should!)
- Firing schedule (Full fuse, slump, fire polish, pot melt, to what target temp)
- How many hours/minutes to complete the firing
- Results

This all may seem like overkill, but it will very much come in handy if 1) your kiln is firing inconsistently and you need to do alittle forensics before calling the kiln repairman and 2) if you don't fire glass often, a lot of time goes by and you forget how you got a desired result, you can just flip back in your notes and repeat what is written down.

HOORAY, I FULL FUSED MY FIRST LOAD, NOW WHAT?

Slumping:

Let's say you full fused assembled components into a size and shape that can fit into a mold, like a 12" x 12" square tray. Your mold should be made of fired clay (I've had luck with 3/8" to 1/4" bisqued terra cotta; with at least 1 hole in the bottom dead center; that has at least 3 coats of kiln wash.) Note that the glass will pick up any texture or brush stroke patterns from the clay or kiln wash, so if you are going for a smooth surface make sure you start out with a smooth mold.

Slumping, in my kiln, occurs between 1320 and 1325F. I place the mold directly on the kiln shelf on a shelf where I know it will fire to that temperature. (Note that sometimes I can do both a fire polish and a slump firing in the same kiln by programming it to 1350F and placing the slumps on the coolest shelves. You will need to experiment with it. I have recently read that molds should sit on posts, but I have never had a problem putting them directly on the shelf. No need to have rigid or thin fire paper on the shelf containing the mold.

Making your own mold:

I have made molds using 3/8" – ¼" thick terra cotta clay of slab construction that I bisque fired. I followed the basic design of store bought molds. These molds have sides that rest on the shelf that are higher than the lowest point of the slump shape so that the sides bear the weight of the mold. Holes are strategically placed in the slump shape area to allow gases to escape. Make sure there is one dead center at the bottom. You will need to add holes if there is a lot of surface area in your slump shape. After bisquing, add at least 3 coats of kiln wash to the mold, I change brush stroke direction each time I apply a layer, 90 degrees to the previous coat. Make sure to reopen the hole with a pin tool if the kiln wash fills it in. For free form shapes I cut out a piece of refractory blanket to sit in the mold and shape it so that the glass will slump into its shape. NOTE: Glass that rests on refractory blanket will have a texture on the side that comes in contact with it and extra scrubbing will be required to clean it.

NEVER EVER try to slump glass that it larger than the mold unless you have cut refractory blanket at least as large as the glass to sit between them. You will break the mold.

You may have to adjust your firing schedule if the following happens:

Thermal shock:

Nothing says despair like opening the kiln after waiting for it to cool completely to find what you expect to be the finished piece broken or shattered in the mold. Time to do a little forensics:

1) If the piece is broken and the edges along the break are SMOOTH, it broke in HEATING up. This means you have to slow down your ramp UP to target temp.
2) If the piece is broken and the edges along the break are SHARP, it broke in the COOLING DOWN, which means you need to slow down your cooling segment.
3) If the piece is broken and the edges along the break are SHARP and you have successfully slumped the same type of glass in the same type of mold with the same firing schedule, it may mean that your fused glass is of uneven thickness; or you mixed COE's and the piece simply pulled apart in the cooling to annoy you.

Chances are using my firing schedules will avoid thermal shock as I've had it happen to me and have made the necessary adjustments already, but every kiln is different, so keep this in mind when you do your forensics.

Salvaging a broken piece:

When facing broken ware instead of finished work, stomp around the studio a few times, swear like a sailor, then get over it and get to work salvaging the piece. If you are completely fed up, just shatter it or cut it up and make lots of jewelry, sell it on Etsy and use the money to buy more supplies. Or throw it in a pot melt, drill a hole in the center, fit it with clockworks and tell time with it. (These sell well on Etsy too.) Whatever you do, do not give up; do not throw that glass away.

This is what I do:

If it is a clean break or in segments that are clean, I put it back in the mold, place the broken pieces as close together as possible, then put Udon rods or linguini noodles over the break, making sure it touches the glass on each side and re-fire to somewhere between slump and full fuse temperature. If you like you can fire it to tack temperature, but it will leave a raised texture where you put the rods. I keep a supply of clear flat linguini noodles in stock for this purpose. Sometimes the break will not be noticeable at all, sometimes it will enhance the piece, sometimes you won't like it but a customer will fall in love with it, sometimes it will come out so cool you will do it on purpose. Don't give up!

Finish work/Cold working:

Glass is finicky and sometimes it will do things not according to plan just to spite you. Sometimes after dozens of firings with consistent results it will over fire just to remind you who's boss, or a piece of dichroic will cause a burr in a piece of jewelry that might catch on clothing or scratch skin. Or, you just want to even out a bulge in a piece of glass you want straight.

Using the grinder:

I fully endorse investing in a glass grinder. They are small, are easy to store, are easy to clean and maintain, can go a long time without changing the grinding bit, and are very straightforward to use. There are just a few simple rules:

1) Protect the area around it from splashes. (I keep mine on a shelf with my drape molds and cover the drape molds with plastic.
2) Have a little dish under the outlet hose to catch drips.
3) Keep the sponge that sits behind the grinding bit wet at all times when in use.
4) If it has one, keep the reservoir full of water at all times when in use.
5) Wear safety glasses and a mask and run your studio air filter.
6) Add water to the grinding bit if a paste forms while grinding
7) Unplug and rinse out the pan under the grinding bit (usually you can pop off a plastic grid that sits just under it with a putty knife) after each use.
8) The grinding bit will last a lot longer than you expect. You have my permission to be cheap about it.

After suiting up, wetting down and covering up, simply turn on the grinder and hold the piece you want ground against the bit. Use light steady pressure. If you are removing a bulge, push it back and forth with even pressure and speed until it is straight. If you are removing a burr, especially at the corners, lightly "kiss" the burr to the grinding bit to remove it.

If your grinding produces permanent scratches on the piece you have 1 of 2 options:

1) If it's a tiny scratch and you are on a very limited financial and time budget (i.e. teaching) you can simply put a lick of clear nail polish on the scratch. Nail polish is as strong as many acrylics and comes in a wide range of colors, so you can even use color to match the piece to cover the scratch.
2) If time and money are no object and you have enough to fill the kiln or are doing a slump firing and have a hot spot in the kiln do a fire polish firing, it will remove the scratch without changing the shape of the piece. Fire polishes usually occur at 1375F, but I have had them successfully fire to 1350F on a hot shelf in a mixed load with slumps.

Other fun handy tools:

• **A precision drill press with diamond circle cutters.** I have picked up affordable ones from **AmericanScienceSurplus.com** ; **Lee Valley** also sells them- these are just suggestions. NOTE: some of the circle cutter bits are too big to fit a precision drill press and need a regular sized drill press.

To cut circles using a drill press: Anytime you manipulate glass with a machine you must keep the glass wet. I use a plastic container full of water with a sponge in it. I rest the glass on top of the sponge, pour a little water on the glass, hold the glass firmly and press the drill onto it. As the drill presses, it submerges the glass, the sponge cushions it and keeps it from drilling through the container. WEAR PROTECTIVE EYEWEAR AND APRON as sometimes the bit punches HARD through the glass and shreds the sponge and everything goes flying. NEVER WEAR GLOVES WHEN OPERATING A DRILL PRESS, they can catch on the equipment and injure fingers and hands.

• **Drills equipped with diamond bits.** It takes finesse and practice, but you can drill holes in glass. I find that drilling the hole before firing helps, as sometimes it does not fill in but if it does it makes a depression that facilitates successful drilling. I have not had a lot of success at drilling holes, but go on YouTube and watch how it's done and practice on scrap glass until you get the hang of it. Note that diamond drill bits are pricey and you can expect to go through a few of them before you are proficient, but basically, place the glass you are working with in a container full of water and a sponge. Rest the glass on the sponge. Wet the glass. Place the drill bit where you want to drill the hole ON AN ANGLE. Fire away with the drill while holding the glass securely, to create the beginnings of a hole, once you have it scored, point the drill straight down and apply pressure until the hole is drilled. This is all much easier said than done. WEAR SAFETY GLASSES.

HANDY TIP: if you are making something you are very attached to or commissioned and feel you might break it, take it to a glass company that specializes in window repair and shower doors, they will be happy to do it for a fee.

• **Dremel™ tools.** Most potters have one. Use diamond bits. Use the container of water/sponge set up. Make sure when working with the Dremel™ the glass is WET and SECURE so that it does not go flying. WEAR SAFETY GLASSES.

• **Glass saws.** There are saws on the market made specifically for cutting glass, equipped with diamond-coated blades. I have never met one that I like. They are very expensive, the ones in my budget are mostly made out of plastic and come with instructions that are indecipherable and unhelpful. They are always either jamming or going off the track requiring constant adjustment. The flywheels and blades break down constantly and are hugely expensive. I really only recommend them for precision and detailed cutting by someone who is very patient, has lots of time on their hands and financially secure. If you get one find one that is made mostly of metal.

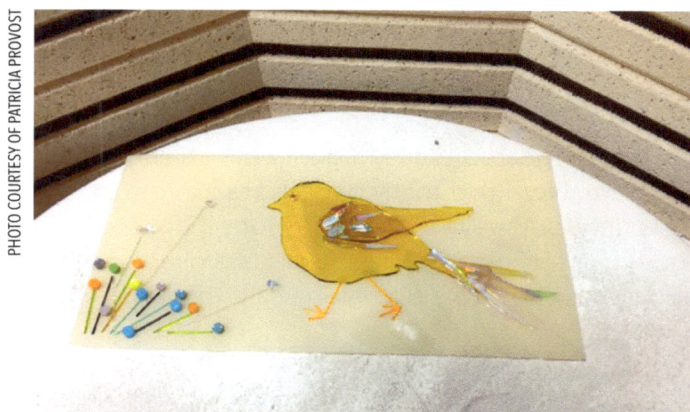

A piece about to be fired:

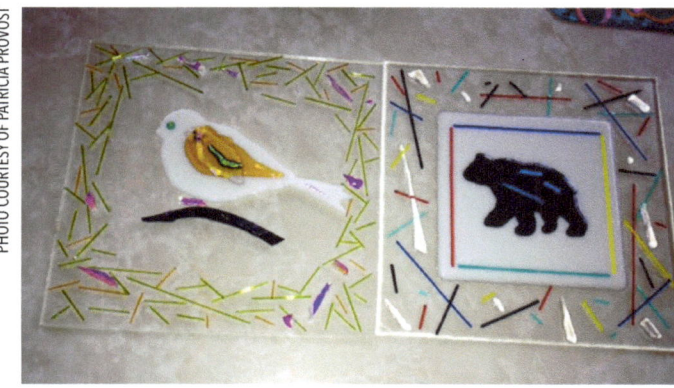

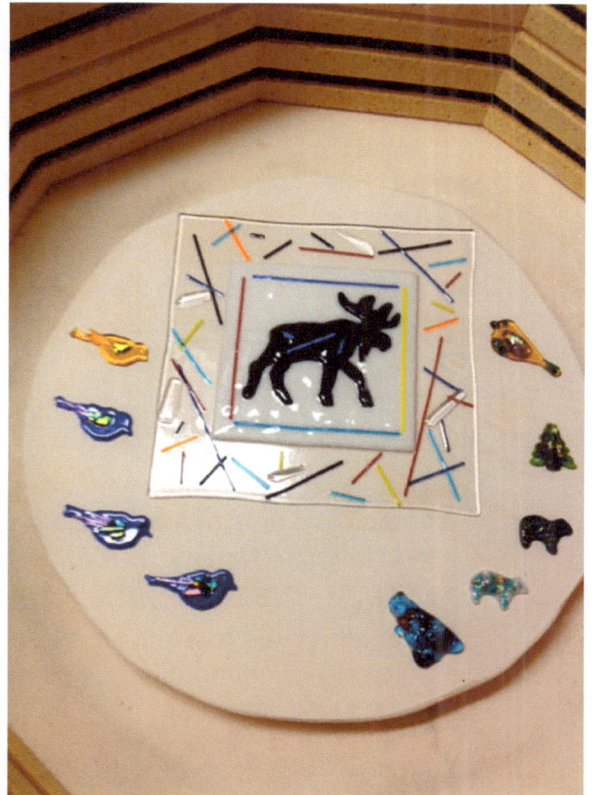

Pieces fresh out of the kiln.

A glass artist who is a master at precision cutting on a glass saw is **Patricia Provost of Cricket Hill Glass**. Above are some of her and her daughter Lauren's creations made using components cut on a glass saw.

Firing metal into glass:

Once you are proficient in the firing basics it's time to expand into firing inclusions in your glass projects. Embedding metal into glass has a wide range of uses. Nichrome wire hooks are most common, but decorating with metal shavings, metal leaf or mica powders can enhance the aesthetics of a piece. Just note that cracks and fissures may develop in the glass around wire or any thick metal inclusions, as the glass tries to contract in cooling around this rigid foreign object. Metals need not be expensive- experiment with what you have on hand- I have even asked the kind folks at the hardware store to empty their key machine grinding shavings into a paper bag for me to take home. Mica powders come in a wide range of colors. You can even experiment by including them into slips, terra sigillata and glazes in your clay practice. Metal leaf are interesting though a little hard to work with. I enjoy using imitation gold leaf- when fired to the correct temperature (I haven't pin pointed it yet but give me time) it turns a wonderful Caribbean blue. My advice is to do a bubble squeeze if you are including metal leaf in your work as it does cause gases that need to escape during firing. One word of advice: do not cover the entire surface area between layers of glass with metal as it will act like flour in a cake pan and the glass will not stick together.

MAKING JEWELRY

There are many glue-on findings on the market geared to fused glasswork, mainly in the form of bails in nickel, gold plate, or silver plate. Note that many people are allergic to nickel so it is best to get the silver plated variety, but they can be pricey for school and bulk budgets. Bails can also be made out of glass by placing 2 layers of glass over refractory rope, leaving enough area at one end to full fuse into a piece. They are tricky but cost effective as you can use scrap glass and refractory board/rope.

To glue on findings:

NOTE: ONLY USE **E6000™ GLUE** AVAILABLE AT CRAFT AND HARDWARE STORES!

Decide in advance where you want to put the finding. Sometimes it looks nice to glue the finding in a non intuitive place, so make sure to try it several different ways, especially for square items- sometimes it looks nice in a diamond or asymmetrical shape achieved by putting the finding on a corner instead of in the middle of a straight edge.

Protect the table top with a piece of paper or cardboard; have an area designated for the pieces to dry without moving them for several hours.

- Make sure the area to be glued is clean.
- Put a small amount of glue (E6000™) on a cotton swab that has been dipped in Everclear™.
- Spread on finding.
- Attach the finding in the desired spot on the back of the piece, pressing firmly. Don't worry if the glue oozes out.
- Lay the piece finding side up where it can dry undisturbed.
- After about 20 minutes you can take a toothpick and prize up any glue that oozed then pull it up with your fingers, it should pull away from the finding.
- Glue will be completely dry in 24 hours. It's fairly easy to remove the finding and clean off the glue before then if you change your mind and want to try again. (use nail polish remover)

For pendants:

Sometimes the backside of pendants may be rough, especially when fired directly onto rigid fiberboard. Pendants with rough backs may pill a sweater, so it's a good idea to coat the back with nail polish to smooth it out. Nail polish is great because if it wears off you can just reapply.

If the piece is clear or translucent bear in mind that it will change to whatever color you are wearing it against, which may cause it to disappear into what you are wearing. You may want to apply silver or gold or some sort of metallic colored nail polish to make the design pop and shimmer. Be creative! Note if you don't like it- just use nail polish remover and try with another color. Have fun! If your piece has scratches or a burr you can touch it up or tone down the sharp burr with nail polish that matches the color of the piece or clear.

For Earrings:

There are 2 different types of earring findings: post and wire hangers. Post is very easy to assemble. Just put glue on the back of the post and glue in the desired area, pressing firmly. Remove oozed glue as described for pendants or just leave it, but let the glue dry completely for at least 24 hours before using. Note that the glue may wear out over time and you may need to reapply but I have only had it fail once.

Wire hanging earrings are alittle more complicated. There is a small bail that must first be glued to the glass. After drying completely you will need to attach the hanger by holding one end with a tweezers and prizing it open with a needle nose plier. (Good eyesight or a jeweler's magnifier is required) Try not to manipulate the wire hanger more than absolutely necessary so that it does not weaken the wire. Be sure to orient the wire hanger so that the front of the glass faces forward otherwise you'll be doing it again! Close the wire as much as possible without using excessive force. If you are like me and lose wire hanger earrings at an alarming rate you may want to go to the drug store and buy "ear nuts" which are little plastic backs to keep them from falling off.

Pins:

Very easy, just glue, press and let dry. Remove excess if necessary.

Bracelets:

Easy again, just glue, press and let dry. Good luck getting it to stay still as you glue each piece.

Ponytail holder:

It's a little tricky to get the glue to go only where you want it. You need to put the elastic loop in the depression in the finding, then glue each flat side of the finding and glue it onto the glass without having the elastic fall out or get glued to the glass. Once you have the finding glued down move the elastic a little to make sure there is not glue on it and that it moves freely in the finding.

For your viewing pleasure I have a tutorial video of how to attach findings described herein.
Go to http://www.lisagw.com

Click on: Login
Enter User name: Student
Enter Password: Jewelry
Click on top left: Jewelry Finding Tutorial

LISA G WESTHEIMER CERAMICS & GLASS   LISAGWCERAMICSNGLASS.ETSY.COM

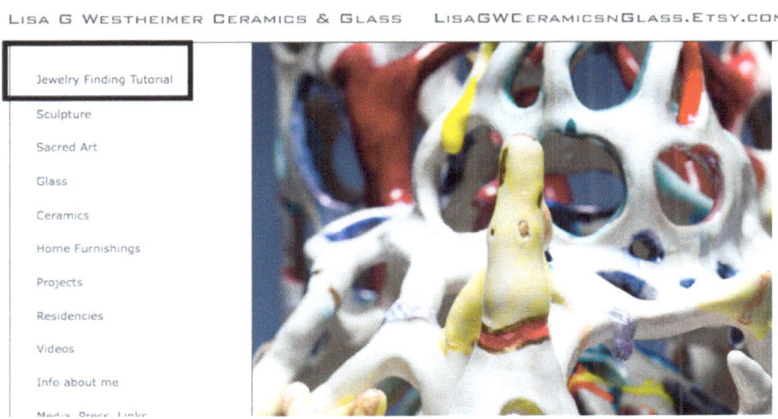

Jewelry Finding Tutorial
Sculpture
Sacred Art
Glass
Ceramics
Home Furnishings
Projects
Residencies
Videos
Info about me
Media, Press, Links

FORENSICS/TROUBLE SHOOTING

The following will help you figure out what went wrong, or what gave you a really cool unexpected result you want to do again:

- **The glass cut beyond the score line:** you used too little or too much pressure in scoring, or there's a flaw in the glass.
- **Pieces come out of kiln with sharp edges:** Either the piece over-fired or you fired it directly onto rigid fiber board and it caught while contracting or both;
- **Single pieces of glass when full fused came out misshapen; hourglass shaped:** this is caused by the fact you fired only 1 sheet of glass with embellishments scattered about. I recommend firing at least 2 layers of glass in a full fuse firing.
- **Full fused pieces have bubbles/grey ash inside:** you used too much glue to hold it together before putting it in the kiln.
- **Pieces develop cracks upon cooling or over time:** you mixed glasses of different COE's.
- **Pieces break or fall apart for no explicable reason:** the piece was not properly annealed.
- **The piece broke in the slump mold and the edges are smooth:** thermal shock in the heating phase, extend your heating rate per hour in the first segment.
- **The piece broke in the slump mold and the edges are sharp:** thermal shock in the cooling phase, extend your cooling rate per hour in the last segment.
- **The full fuse piece is misshapen along the edge; i.e. bulging:** glass components were placed too close to the edge prior to full fusing.
- **Tack fired pieces of the same COE fell apart after cooling:** The pieces did not have enough time to fuse together- extend the hold time at target temperature.
- **A square piece came out round in full fuse:** it over fired.
- **A full fuse piece came out rough textured:** it over fired
- **Dichroic glass came out grey:** it over fired
- **Dichroic glass did not come out:** it was fired upside down
- **Glass components did not sink into iridescent glass in full fuse:** the iridescent glass was placed metal side up.
- **Fired glass is cloudy:** glass was not made specifically for fusing, i.e. not "hot glass" or "fusible glass."

INCORPORATING GLASS AND CLAY INTO ONE FORM:

Now that you have become proficient in firing glass in your clay kiln it is time to expand your horizons. Most clay and glass artists are naturally curious and want to know *what would happen if????* Asking those questions is what got me into glass working in the first place so here are a few things I have learned along the way:

Using glass in glaze:

Since glass is mostly silica it is a natural glaze. Getting it to fit into a formula is tricky. Best to use only on decorative pieces, as it will craze and you don't want to kill off your customer base by having them to eat or drink glass fragments that has broken off the bottom of a bowl or cup. In particular I like to use glass in raku firings- I just throw it in around the time the glaze has matured and have it melt like cheese on a pizza before removing to the reduction cans. Make sure to throw it onto the glazed portion of the piece so it will stick.

I also incorporate glass in pieces during multi-firing. I will add glass inclusions to sculptures or decorative objects and fire from cone 018 to 015 depending on the amount of fusion/texture I want. Sometimes the glass has trouble sticking to a glaze, mille fiori in particular, so I add a dab of a paste of borax and water to help it stick.

A clay artist who uses glass regularly in his clay work is **Steven Branfman**, who was kind enough to share some images of him and his work.

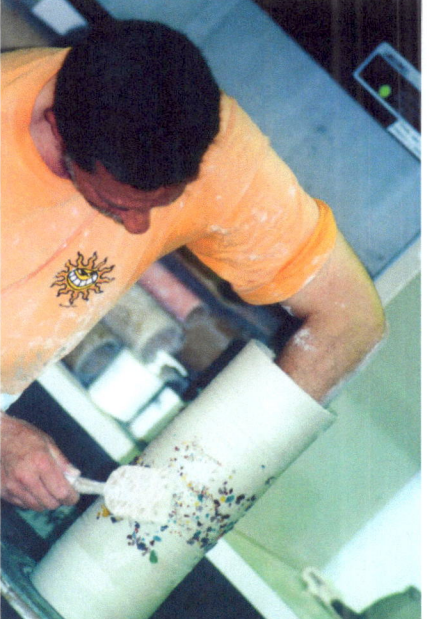

PHOTO COURTESY OF STEVEN BRANFMAN

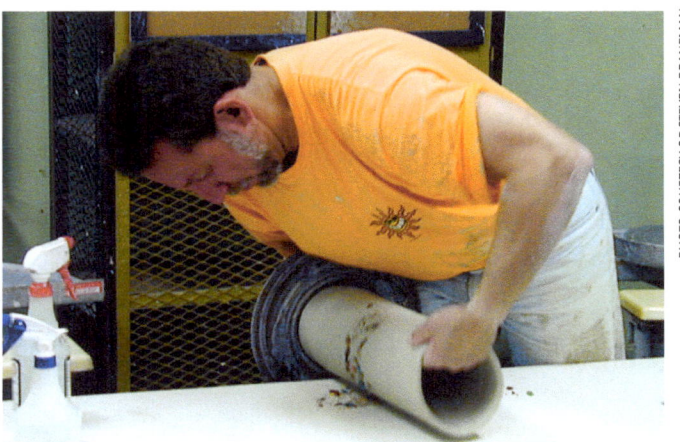

PHOTO COURTESY OF STEVEN BRANFMAN

Paddles the glass firmly into the cylinder of clay.

He impresses broken found glass by rolling it into a greenware.

Then expands the cylinder into the desired shape.

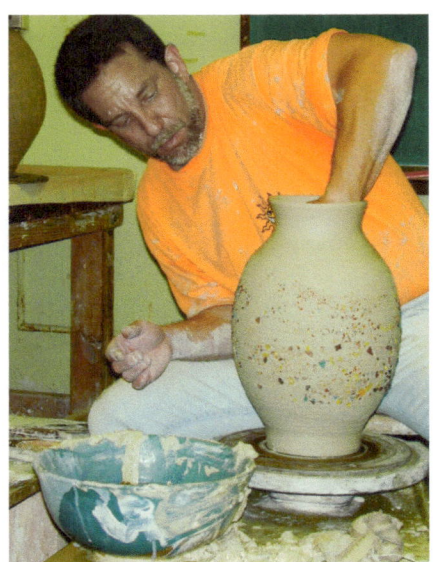

PHOTO COURTESY OF STEVEN BRANFMAN

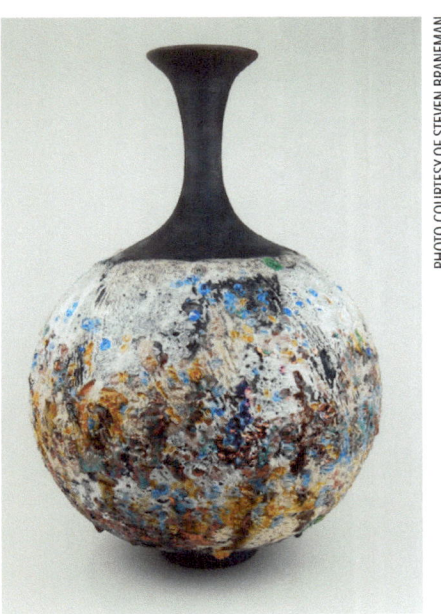

PHOTO COURTESY OF STEVEN BRANFMAN

He then raku fires them with stunning results.

SOME EXAMPLES OF FIRING GLASS ONTO CERAMIC FORMS

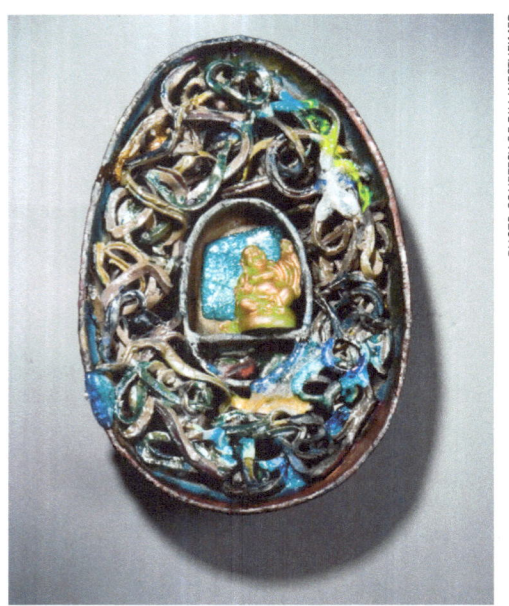

PHOTO COURTESY OF BILL WESTHEIMER

Happiness
2005

Adding glass in Raku and Wood firing

◄ Raku:

Glass and metal were thrown onto this piece in the raku kiln just as the glaze matured. The pieces were removed from the kiln once the glass started to melt. Note the glass needs to fall onto a glazed area to stick.

Wood Fire: ►

In this example, ground bottle glass was placed on the floor of the sculpture prior to loading it in the wood fire kiln.

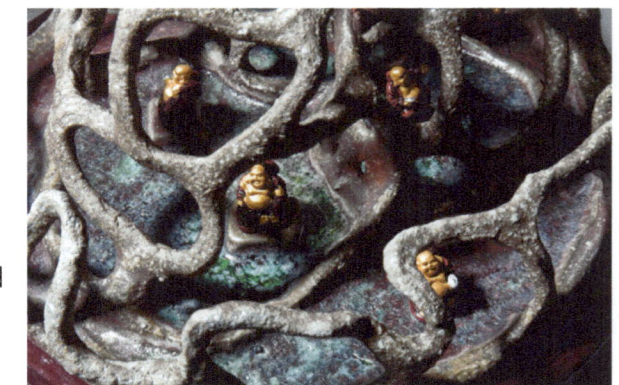

PHOTO COURTESY OF BILL WESTHEIMER

Hotei Hideaway
2011

Multi-firing in an electric kiln:

These sculptures were fired several times, the first being bisque, the last to add lusters. In all 3 cases, glass was added in the 2nd to last firing.

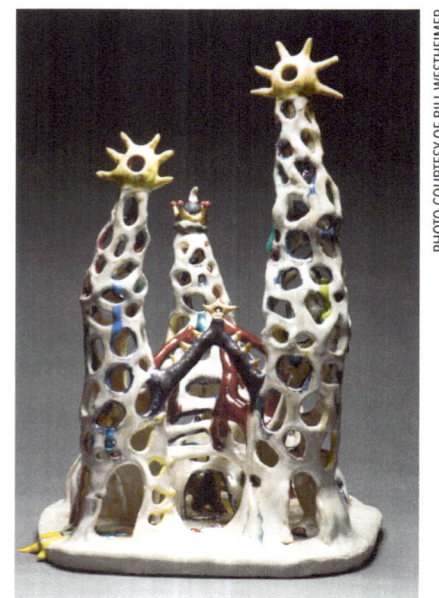

PHOTO COURTESY OF BILL WESTHEIMER

Holy Innocents
2008

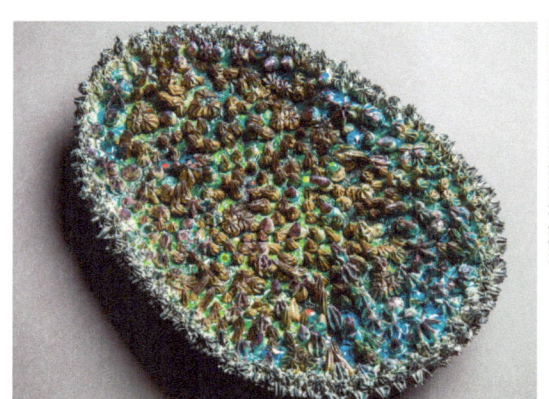

PHOTO COURTESY OF BILL WESTHEIMER

Haeckel microcosm-Green
2015

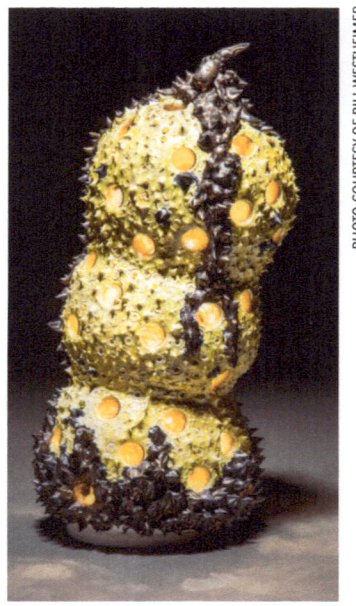

PHOTO COURTESY OF BILL WESTHEIMER

Sponge Lamp
2016

Using glass in a clay frame:

Make the frame before the glass insert so you don't have to worry about shrinkage rates. The easiest way to incorporate glass into a clay object is to create a frame out of clay, make a ledge all the way around the opening and glue glass onto the ledge. The trick is to get the glass the correct size. Err on the side of it being too big as you can always grind it down. If it is a little small or uneven and has gaps don't despair, strategic gluing will take care of the problem.

Pictured at right is an example of a clay frame with a ledge along the interior.

This is the back of the frame, glue will be applied to the ledge and the glass will be placed over it.

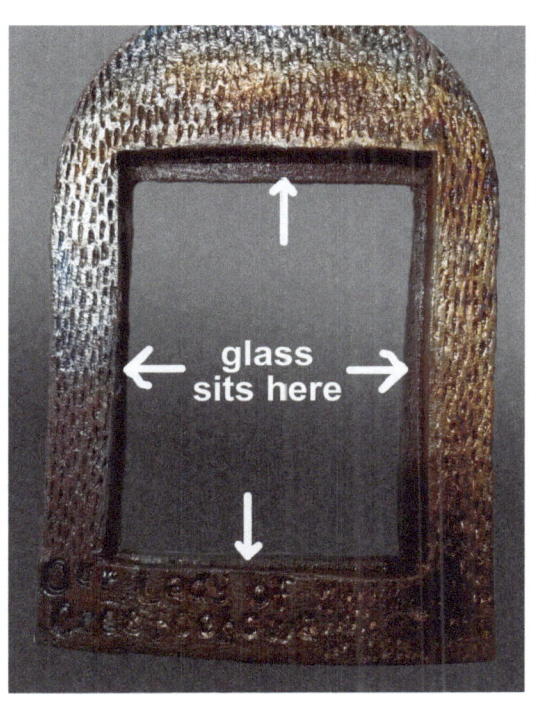

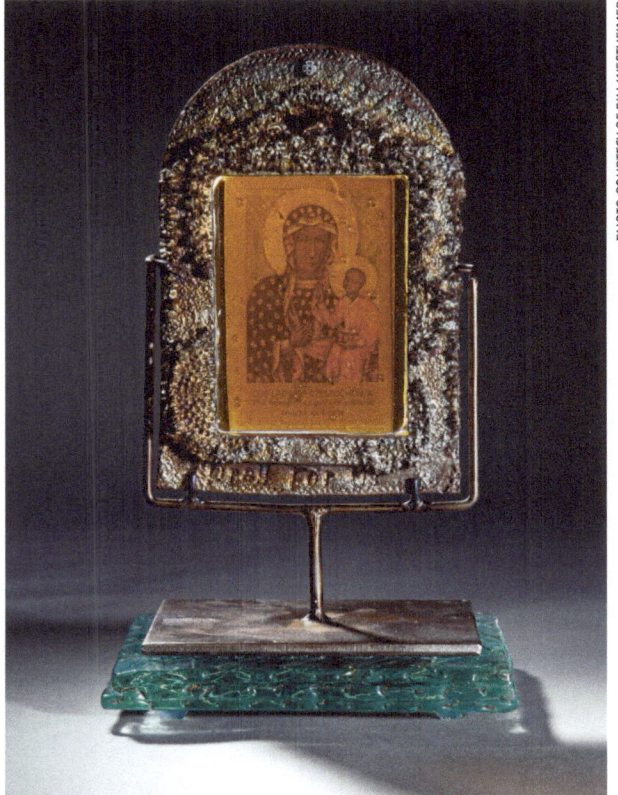

*Our Lady of Czestochowa
(Pray for Us), front*

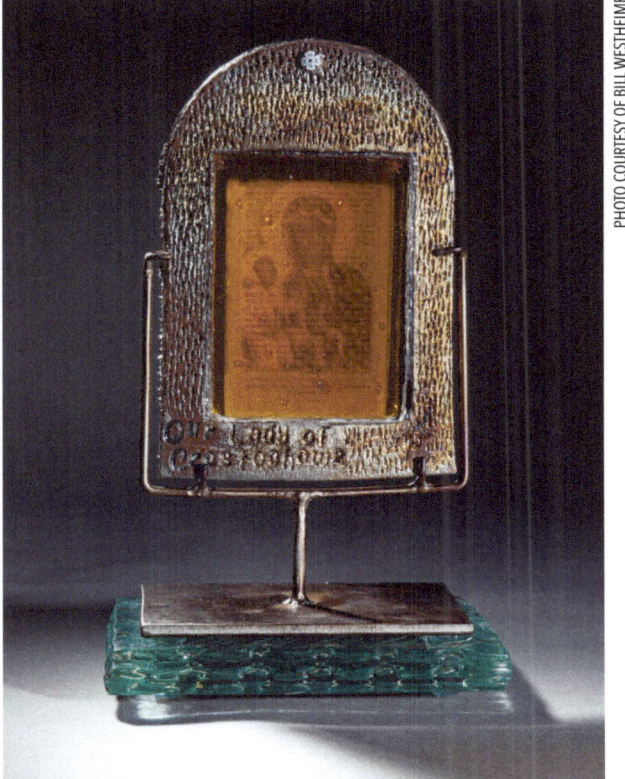

*Our Lady of Czestochowa
(Pray for Us), back*

Using glass to follow the shape of a curved form:

I have always been fascinated by containers. The bulk of my aesthetic practice involves making them out of clay and glass. My first proclivity is to throw a form on the wheel then add glass windows. Making straight forms would be way too easy. Having a straight piece of glass in a curved opening seems like cheating. So how to get the glass to follow the curve of the clay form?

In addition to slumping glass, it can also be draped. It's not as easy as slumping, as the glass has to balance on top of the drape mold in the kiln, but it can be done. My experiments led me to throwing a form, trimming and drying to leather hard, then using a knife to cut where I want the openings WITHOUT DISCARDING OR DISTORTING THE CUT OUTS. It is tricky to clean up the cuts on both outside and inside the form and to ensure the glass has something to sit in for gluing, but it can be done. I carefully remove the cut outs, one-by-one, clean the edges of both the cut out and the opening, poke a hole in the center of the cut out with a pin tool then re-insert the cut out into the opening, pressing gently to get a good fit. I do this to every cut out. It is essential that the cut outs dry inserted into the form to maintain a good fit. If you are afraid the cutouts will fuse to the piece in the bisque paint some wax resist or put corn starch on the edges of the cut outs before re-inserting. Be aware they may fall out during drying, at some point you may have to hold them in with masking tape or other ingenious devices potters are so good at, like chopsticks and sponges.

After bisquing, remove the cut outs; kiln wash, cut your glass to fit then fire them to slump temperature ON TOP OF the cutouts. Note that it is possible, and actually my preference; to use glass I have embellished and fused before draping into the required shape. After they are fired you can grind them to fit and glue in.

Here are some examples:

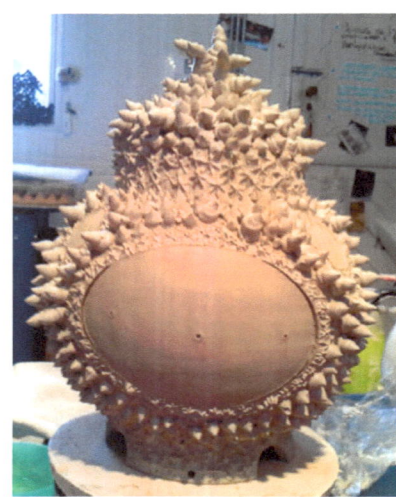 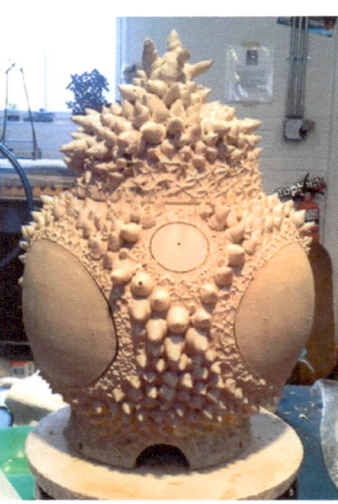 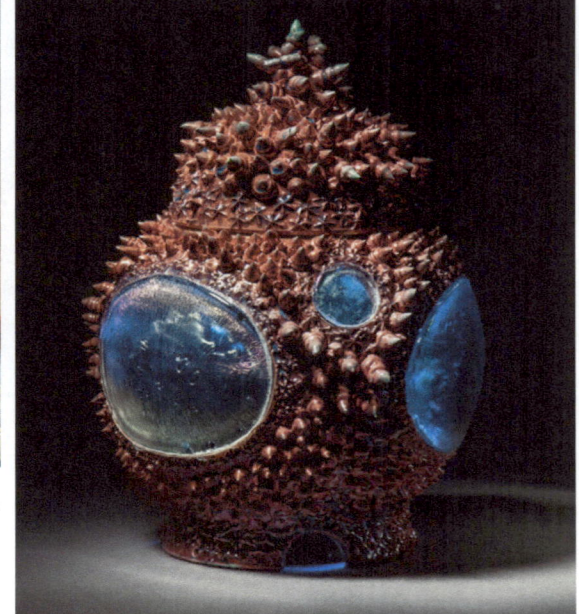

Go Away
Tokens: 2012. Urn/Sculpture: 2014
Luster fired stoneware with fused glass and LED lighting
13" h x 9" w x 9" w (irregular)

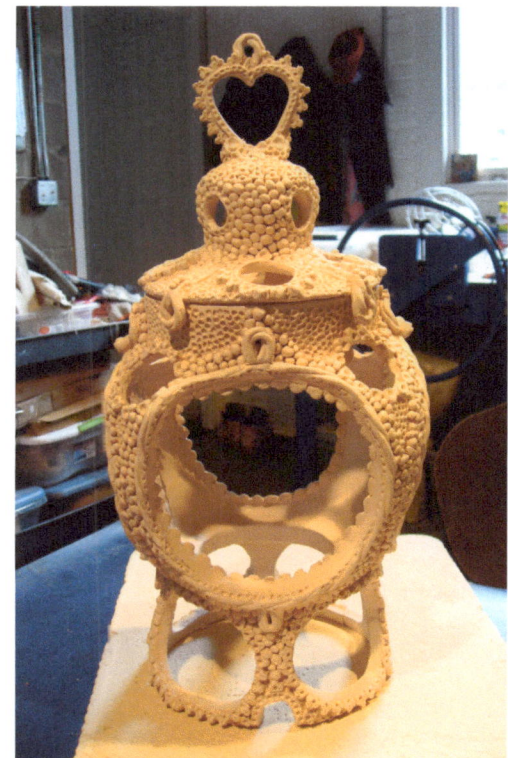

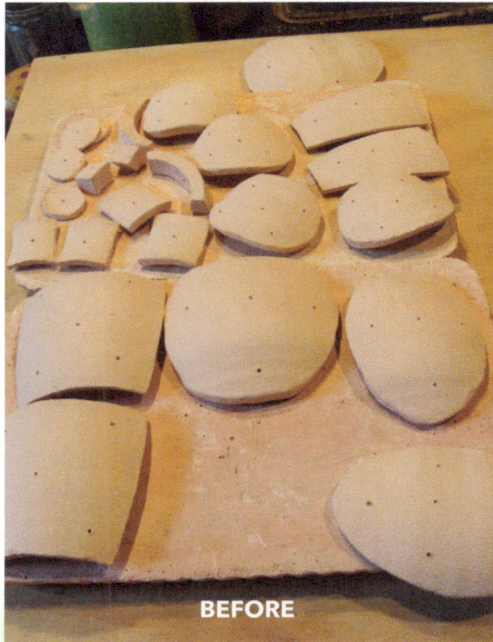

BEFORE

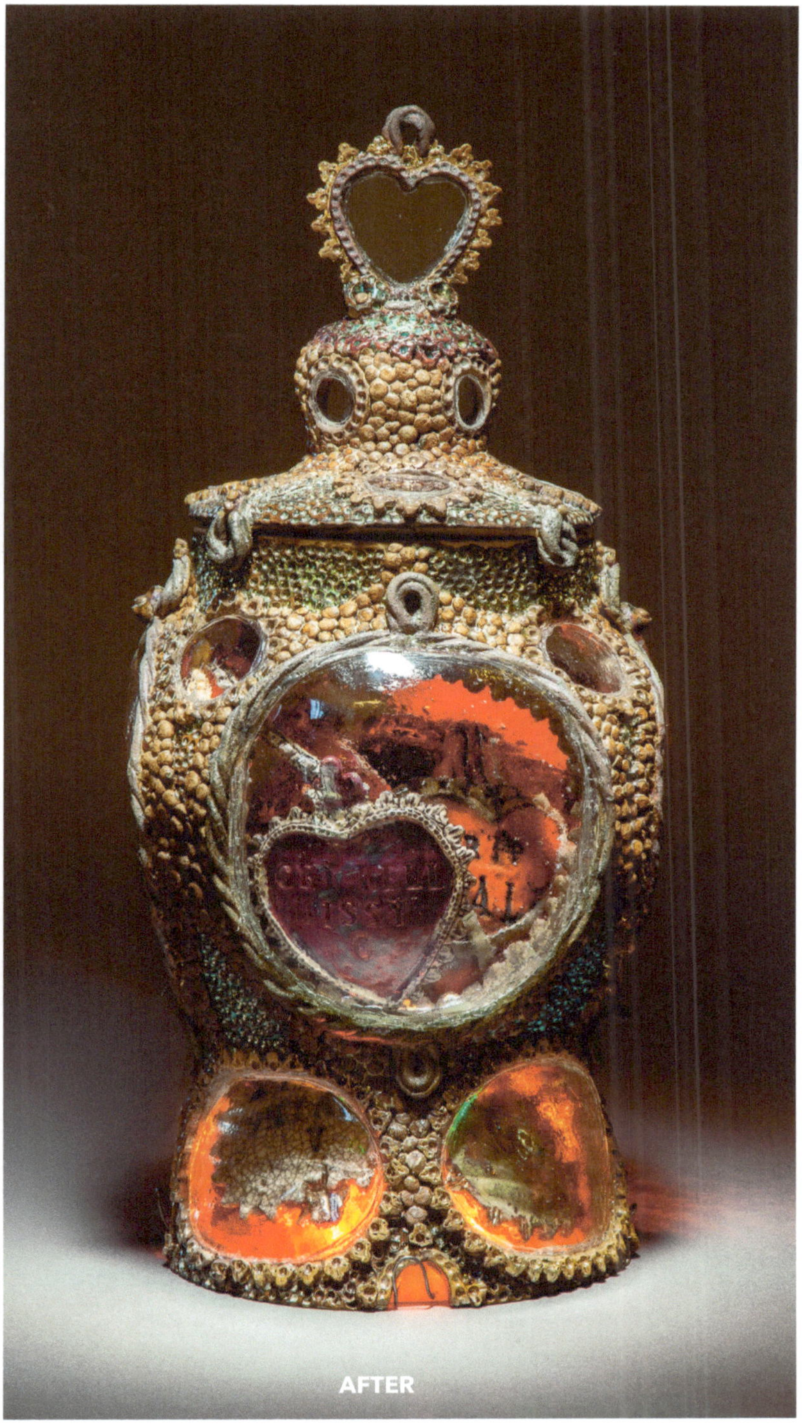

AFTER

Private Prayers
Tokens: 2012
Urn/Sculpture: 2014
Luster fired stoneware with fused glass and LED lighting
15-1/4" h x 6-1/2" w x 6-1/2" d

STRATEGIC GLUING

Sometimes no matter how hard you try, the glass does not fit well. It is too big on one side and too small on another. Patient grinding will get the glass to fit better. Just keep grinding and placing it into the opening, and repeat until it is as close as can be. If there is a gap, the magic of E6000™ glue, Everclear™ and a cotton swab/Q-tip™ will save the day.

It is possible to fill in gaps with E6000™ glue without it oozing out all over the place. The glue is very easy to manipulate with a cotton swab/Q-tip™ dipped in Everclear™ (grain alcohol.) Note that if you do not have access to Everclear™ try denatured alcohol. Isopropyl alcohol or nail polish remover doesn't work as well.

The trick is to be very patient. The glue needs to be a certain consistency: between fresh and almost dry to work with.

It is recommended to use an E6000™ tube with a pointy applicator for this task.

- Place the glass in the opening.

- Glue the glass in where it fits, leaving the edges with the gaps for last.

- In the area where there is a gap: place a thin line of glue set back a bit from the edge of the glass.

- Let the glue set up for about 5 minutes, maybe more. You may have to secure the glass into the opening somehow (try supporting it with a chop stick or some similar device or masking tape.)

- Once the glue has set up, gently prod it down to the outer edge of the glass with a cotton swab soaked in Everclear™. You will find that it is easily moved and manipulated after the glue has set up a bit.

- Place a bead of glue behind the bead you just moved and repeat the process. Every time you prod the glue towards the gap it will get closer to the edge of the ceramic opening. Once there is just a minimal gap, you can close it with a bead of glue. Keep it supported until it sets up for at least 15 to 20 minutes. You can clean up any excess glue as you would working with jewelry findings.

At right is an example of strategic gluing:

The glass didn't exactly fit; in fact there was a significant gap that the glue filled; see arrow in bottom picture.

NOTE: be advised that E6000™ shrinks when as it dries. Keep that in mind as I have had single thickness glass fracture from the stress of the glue shrinking around it. If your glass has a large surface area make sure you are using a piece of glass made of 2 fused layers.

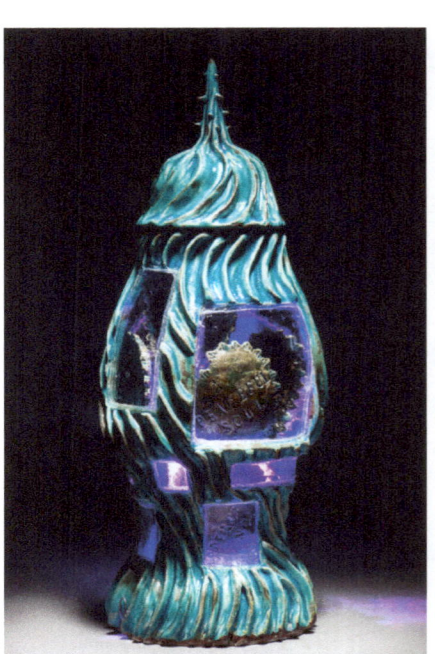

PHOTOS COURTESY OF BILL WESTHEIMER

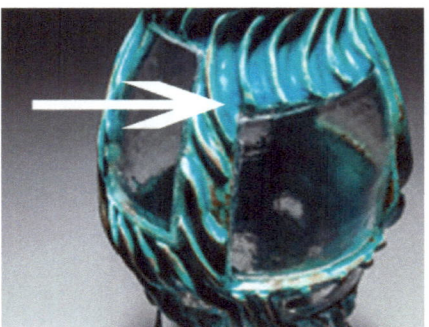

A Peaceful Soul
Tokens: 2012, Urn/Sculpture: 2014
Luster fired stoneware with fused glass and LED lighting

SUMMARY

So there you have it, my entire bag of tricks for glass working in a clay studio, firing glass in a clay kiln, incorporating glass in ceramic forms. I hope you use this information not as Gospel truth, but as a springboard to launching your own glass/clay practice. Consider it a journey of discovery and try to maintain a spirit of learning and adventure, especially for those times when you have done everything according to your meticulous notes and things still go wrong. You may find yourself back to the drawing board more often than you like for no reason other than unlike clay, which will be faithful to you until the end like a dog, the glass is disrespecting you like a cat.

On your glassmaking journey, you may find that the skills acquired enhance your clay practice. On my journey I have found that working on a small scale with precision tools to maneuver small bits of glass into place has given me more manual dexterity and enhanced my detail making in clay.

SUGGESTED READING

Since I am self-taught in glass fusing, and my explorations began prior to the popularity of instructional videos on the Internet, I depended on books to teach me much of what I know. I found the following reading material to be invaluable in my glass practice and I love having them in my studio for easy reference:

Kiln Firing Glass- Glass Fusing Book One, Boyce Lundstrum

Glass Casting & Moldmaking- Glass Fusing Book Three, Boyce Lundstrum

The Joy of Fusing, Randy Wardell

Introduction to Glass Fusing, Petra Kaiser

Contemporary Fused Glass, Brad Walker

ACKNOWLEDGEMENTS

Many thanks to the following people for sharing their time, talent, images and expertise for development of this book: Patricia Provost of Cricket Hill Glass, Oak Ridge, NJ; Kate Dowd of Glassroots Gallery, Newark, NJ; Don Abel of Morton Glass Works Inc, Morton, Illinois; Steven Branfman of The Potters Shop and School, Newton, Massachusetts; Richard Sheinaus of Gotham Design, Montclair, NJ; and Bill Westheimer of Petey Pie Press, West Orange, NJ.

GLOSSARY OF TERMS

The following are terms found throughout this manual; many of them are shorthand for processes or materials common to the glass fusing process, an asterisk is placed at definitions to denote from where I learned them.

Annealing: A firing process integral to the glass firing process to prevent breakage, wherein the kiln is cooled to quartz inversion temperature and held for a specific time prior to cooling to room temperature.

COE: coefficient of expansion/contraction: "A number indicating the percentage of change in length, per degree Centigrade change in temperature."*

Dichroic glass: Opaque fusible glass that changes color in the light.

Findings: Components, usually of metal, typically bails, wires, pins, and etc. that are glued onto or melted into fused glass used to create jewelry.

Firing schedule: The temperature rate of rise and fall and hold times required to achieve specific results in the fusing of glass.

Float glass: Sheet glass made by pouring liquid glass over molten tin.*

Frit: Bits of glass used to embellish fused glass creations. Made of broken glass in various grits from fine to coarse.

Full Fuse: The temperature at which layers of glass or glass components melt to form one cohesive layer of glass.

Fusible glass: aka hot glass; glass created and designed for melting/fusing when heated to specific temperature.

Fused glass: Layers of glass that have been melted in a kiln or forge or lampworked to form one cohesive piece of glass.

Iridescent glass: Transparent fusible glass that changes color in the light.

Mille Fiori/Murini: Originally made in Murano, Italy, long rods of glass composed of multi-colored, multi-layers that when sliced form a distinct pattern. Also known as Moretti.

Morton System™: A cutting system designed by *Morton Glass Works* consisting of components and bars fitting into a grid system to assist in cutting specific shapes of glass.

Noodles/Stringers: Fusible glass rods of varying lengths and thicknesses, usually of a single color.

Pebbles: Drops or blobs of glass that when full fused form a circle.

Quartz inversion: The reversible point at which quartz crystals change in the glass, glaze or ceramic firing process, usually between 800F – 1000F.

Refractory blanket: aka ceramic fiber blanket; a reusable soft flexible material made to withstand high temperature, used in glass fusing and slumping to shape glass as it becomes soft in the kiln, and to keep it from sticking to shelves, furniture and molds.

Refractory paper: aka fiber paper aka thin fire paper; like refractory blanket in that it resists glass sticking to shelves, but it single use and paper thin.

Rigid fiber paper/board: Thin, rigid board of refractory ceramic properties placed between shelves and glass to keep the glass from sticking. Can be reused until it becomes brittle.

Slump: The result of firing at a temperature that softens glass enough to sink into a mold designed to give it a specific shape.

Slump mold: The mold in which a piece of glass rests on in the kiln, which, upon heating to softening, will give the glass a specific shape.

Tack/dimensional/contour fire: The result of firing at a temperature lower than full fuse that fuses the glass layers/components together but retains the shape of each individual piece.

Tectonics: "geological structural features as a whole"** used to explain the molecular shifts and changes during quartz inversion and the importance of annealing and knowing the coefficient of expansion of glass before melting.

Window glass: Typically made in the float process where liquid glass is poured over molten tin to form a sheet that is smooth on both sides. *

*Quoted from/paraphrased from *The Glassery* section of *Kiln Firing Glass, Glass Fusing Book One*, by Boyce Lundstrom

**Definition of "tectonic" by Miriam Webster Dictionary, *https://www.merriam-webster.com/dictionary/tectonic*

HELPFUL LINKS & WEBSITES

The links below are all available at:

WWW.PETEYPIEPRESS.COM/OUR-BOOKS/GLASS-FUSING-IN-A-CLAY-KILN/LINKS/

Steve Branfman: www.thepottersshop.com/steven-branfman

Bill Westheimer: www.billwest.com

Lisa G Westheimer: www.lisagw.com

Petey Pie Press: www.PeteyPiePress.com

Gotham Design: www.gothamdesign.com

Glass Roots Gallery: www.glassroots.org/

Peters Valley School of Craft: www.petersvalley.org

Montclair Art Museum: www.montclairartmuseum.org

Morton Glass Works: www.mortonglass.com

My videos mentioned in my bio:

Strike Firing Lusterware with Lisa G Westheimer: www.amazon.com/Strike-Firing-Lusterware-Lisa-Westheimer/dp/B013FA05ZG/ref=sr_1_1?keywords=lisa+westheimer&qid=1580319900&sr=8-1

Smoke Firing, Horsehair BBQ: https://www.amazon.com/Smoke-Firing-Horsehair-Lisa-Westheimer/dp/B013FA03IA/ref=sr_1_3?keywords=lisa+westheimer&qid=1580767837&sr=8-3

FIRING SCHEDULES

FOR SYSTEM 96 AND COE 96 COMPATIBLE GLASS

Glass full Fuse Firing Schedule

SEGMENT	RAMP TEMP/HR	GOAL TEMP	HOLD TIME
1	325 F	1000 F	10 minutes
2	600	1465-1484	20
3	9999	960	50
4	150	700	10

(target temperature about cone 015)

Glass Slumping Firing Schedule

SEGMENT	RAMP TEMP/HR	GOAL TEMP	HOLD TIME
1	325 F	1000 F	10 minutes
2	600	1320-1325	25
3	9999	960	50
4	150	400	0

(target temperature about cone 018)

Glass Tack/Contour/Dimensional Firing Schedule
(bonds glass together but leaves detail of individual pieces)

SEGMENT	RAMP TEMP/HR	GOAL TEMP	HOLD TIME
1	325 F	1000 F	10 minutes
2	600	1400	20
3	9999	960	50
4	150	700	10

(target temperature about cone 016 or less)

Glass Fire Polish
(brightens work and removes scratches after grinding and finish work performed)

SEGMENT	RAMP TEMP/HR	GOAL TEMP	HOLD TIME
1	325 F	1000 F	10 minutes
2	600	1350-1375	20
3	9999	960	50
4	150	700	10

(target temperature about cone 017)

FOR FLOAT, WINDOW, PANE, BOTTLE GLASS:

Glass Full Fuse/Slump Firing Schedule

SEGMENT	RAMP TEMP/HR	GOAL TEMP	HOLD TIME
1	325 F	1000 F	10 minutes
2	600	1500-1536	10
3	9999	960	50
4	150	700	10

(target temperature about cone 013)

POT-MELTS (Make sure to protect your shelves very well!)

SEGMENT	RAMP TEMP/HR	GOAL TEMP	HOLD TIME
1	600	1650F	90 minutes
2	9999	960	60

FIRING LOG

#Th= #firings since thermocouple replacement

#E= # firings since element replacement

#TH	#E	DATE	TYPE OF FIRING	TARGET TEMP	HOLD	FIRING TIME	RESULTS

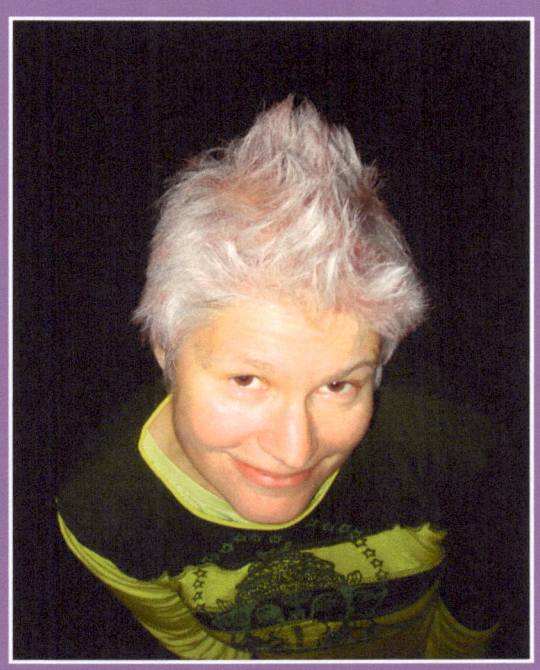

LISA G WESTHEIMER is a full time artist living and working in West Orange, New Jersey, USA. She has a Masters in Studio Arts (Ceramics) from Montclair State University, Montclair, NJ. She teaches glass fusing and ceramics at the Yard School of Art at Montclair Art Museum, Peters Valley School of Craft, Layton, NJ and privately. Her work has been displayed in venues across the United States. In addition to this book, she is author of two instructional videos Strike Firing Luster Ware with Lisa G Westheimer and Smoke Firing, Horsehair BBQ available on Amazon.com.

NOTES